THE CLOTHING WORKERS OF
GREAT BRITAIN

THE CLOTHING WORKERS OF GREAT BRITAIN

S.P. DOBBS

Routledge
Taylor & Francis Group

LONDON AND NEW YORK

First published in 1928

Reprinted in 2006 by
Routledge
2 Park Square, Milton Park, Abingdon, Oxon, OX14 4RN

Routledge is an imprint of Taylor & Francis Group

Transferred to Digital Print 2010

© 1928 S.P. Dobbs

British Library Cataloguing in Publication Data
A CIP catalogue record for this book
is available from the British Library

The Clothing Workers of Great Britain
ISBN 0-415-37992-X (volume)
ISBN 0-415-37990-3 (subset)
ISBN 0-415-28619-0 (set)

Routledge Library Editions: Economic History

STUDIES IN ECONOMICS AND POLITICAL SCIENCE

Edited by

THE DIRECTOR OF THE LONDON SCHOOL OF ECONOMICS
AND POLITICAL SCIENCE

No. 96 in the series of Monographs by writers connected with the
London School of Economics and Political Science

THE CLOTHING WORKERS OF
GREAT BRITAIN

THE
CLOTHING WORKERS
OF GREAT BRITAIN

By

S. P. DOBBS, B.A.

*Formerly Lecturer in Economics in the Universities of
Toronto and Sheffield*

WITH AN INTRODUCTION BY

THE RT. HON. SIDNEY WEBB,
LL.B., M.P.

LONDON
GEORGE ROUTLEDGE & SONS LTD.
BROADWAY HOUSE: 68-74 CARTER LANE, E.C.
1928

LIST OF ABBREVIATIONS

The following abbreviations of the full titles of certain bodies have frequently been used throughout the following chapters :—

A.L.M.T. Association of London Master Tailors.

A.S.T. & T. Amalgamated Society of Tailors and Tailoresses

L.E.A. London Employers' Association.

N.F.M.T. National Federation of Merchant Tailors.

T. & G.W.T.U. Tailors' and Garment Workers' Trade Union.

CONTENTS

		PAGE
AUTHOR'S PREFACE		ix
INTRODUCTION BY THE RT. HON. SIDNEY WEBB, LL.B., M.P.		xi

CHAPTER

I.	INTRODUCTORY	1
II.	THE CLOTHING TRADES	10
III.	THE LOCALIZATION OF THE INDUSTRY . . .	33
IV.	WAGE REGULATION AND THE TRADE BOARDS .	83
V.	THE WAGE LEVEL AND METHODS OF WAGE PAYMENT	107
VI.	TRADE UNIONS	125
VII.	EMPLOYERS' ASSOCIATIONS	146
VIII.	APPRENTICESHIP AND THE PROBLEM OF RECRUITMENT.	161
IX.	THE DECLINE OF HOMEWORK AND SWEATING. GENERAL REVIEW OF CONDITIONS IN THE INDUSTRY	172
	BIBLIOGRAPHY	203
	APPENDIX I. NUMBERS ENGAGED IN THE CLOTHING TRADES	205
	APPENDIX II. EARNINGS	207
	APPENDIX III. METHODS OF WAGE-PAYMENT .	209
	APPENDIX IIIA. EXAMPLE OF 'LOG' RATES. .	209
	APPENDIX IV. METHODS OF WORK IN THE RETAIL BESPOKE TAILORING TRADES . . .	212
	INDEX	215

AUTHOR'S PREFACE

THIS study of the British Clothing Trades was undertaken under the auspices of the Ratan Tata Foundation (University of London) and represents an attempt to do two things. The first is to describe the present-day structure and localization of the Clothing Industry in Great Britain. The second is to compare existing conditions in the industry with those which prevailed some twenty years ago and to determine the causes to which the changes which have taken place are due. Information has been obtained partly from official government sources, partly from books and from the pages of trade publications and the records of trade associations and trade unions, but in the main from personal interviews with employers, government officials, trade union leaders, ordinary working men and women, and others connected in one way or another with the industry. To all these, too numerous to mention by name, my indebtedness is chiefly due.

In particular I wish to express my thanks to Mr C. M. Lloyd for constant advice in the preparation of my manuscript, to Mr J. J. Mallon for giving me the valuable introductions without which the investigation could not have been satisfactorily carried out, to Mr Frank Popplewell, Professor Hobhouse and Professor Tillyard for assistance in connection with the chapter on Trade Boards, and to the officials of the Tailors' and Garment Workers' Trade Union and of the Amalgamated Society of Tailors and Tailoresses for giving me access to their records. Finally I have to acknowledge the constant help and encouragement received from my wife at all stages of the investigation.

S. P. DOBBS.

BIRMINGHAM,
12th July 1928.

INTRODUCTION

By Sidney Webb

The organization and condition of the Clothing Trades in Great Britain have been more than once described; but the peculiarity of this useful little study is that the subject is dealt with from the viewpoint of the industry being actually, to-day, in process of rapid disintegration and reorganization. In every centre of the industry, and in almost every section of it, what is most manifest is the continuous transformation that is taking place, even whilst it is being observed. How interesting we should find to-day a contemporary study of the changes in cotton spinning in the Manchester area between 1780 and 1800; or of the quick but gradual absorption of the mass of the bootmaking industry by the power-driven factories of 1850-70; or of the entry into paper-making of the new mills filled with the machinery of 1860-80! Since Charles Kingsley wrote *Cheap Clothes and Nasty*, fourscore years ago, the Clothing Trades have been, in Great Britain, in a chronic state of " Industrial Revolution," out of which neither " normalcy " nor stability has yet emerged. With the continual developments, both of machines and of motive power, have been successively combined (1) sensational changes in the application of Division of Labour and Team-work until no fewer than seventy operatives may be united in the making of one " lounge suit "; (2) no less subversive substitutions of one material for another, so that leather and wool and linen and cotton—and now artificial silk—are made to supply, in turn, the substance of most of our body-coverings; and, possibly most revolutionary of all (3) the capricious changes

xi

of fashion, now being reinforced by hygienic alterations in habits, which are not only greatly reducing the quantity of the clothes that we wear, but also, so far as more than half of us are concerned, are practically abandoning the very idea of " fit," on which the highly-skilled dressmaker or tailor of old bestowed so consummate an artistry. It is the effects particularly as manifesting themselves during the last few years of these continuing transformations of the Clothing Trades—alike on the location of the various sections of the industry ; on the processes which these sections employ ; on the employers themselves, and their enterprises ; and on the different grades and kinds of manual workers, their earnings and their conditions—of which Mr Dobbs here gives us a summary picture. A generation ago the picture would have been very different. The next generation will—we may guess—witness changes at least as great. This little book attempts only a snapshot of the present.

Underlying all the changes in the Clothing Trades, as in other industries, we see one invariable feature which may be either cause or effect, or mere concomitant. More and more of the work of supplying the home and the family ceases to be undertaken directly by the members thereof. These, whether men or women, devote themselves increasingly to their specialized work as professionals, in order to earn money with which they purchase, " ready-made," not clothes only, but also practically all their foodstuffs, their toys and other means of recreation—I had almost added their religion and their politics ! Less and less do we rely on the " home-made " article, from bread and cakes and coats and skirts up to amusement and education and religious observances. It is not " fifty-seven " varieties of these things that are nowadays in the market, but fifty-seven thousand varieties. The home-baked loaf ; the home-made dress ; the home-wash ; the home-built toy ; the game, the lesson, the recreation, the

religious observances of the fireside circle, all of which demanded the expenditure of personal time and thought are
more and more superseded, in all grades of society, by the
corresponding product of other people's enterprise, which we
purchase at the price of part of our vocational earnings. And
this development has been proceeding for several centuries.
The peculiarity of the present age is only the acceleration of
the pace. Men—and latterly women also—nowadays make
less at home than any former generation did, work more
abroad, get their income even more exclusively in the form
of currency ; and accordingly adopt the method of purchase
for the acquisition of most of the commodities and services
that they consume. In Continental Europe this tendency has
not yet gone so far as in Britain ; in the United States it has
gone much farther. We are becoming a nation of vocationally
specialized producers, none of us " shooting for the pot," but
always for the market ; dependent for everything that we
need upon the uninterrupted circulation of the resulting commodities and services, all of them produced for other persons'
consumption ; a circulation governed for the most part by
the " cash nexus," but—let us not forget—notably during the
past half-century, also by the extraordinary and continuous
growth both of the Consumers' Co-operative Movement and of
deliberately organized collective services of a public character.

Whatever we may think of the disadvantages attendant on
the substitution of " shop-goods " for " home-made " articles,
the fact must not be ignored that this substitution has brought
to the nation the economic gain of a relatively enormous
increase per head of population in the amount of commodities
and services enjoyed. Family production for domestic use
had the drawback of being always a scanty production, small
in amount, and narrowly restricted in variety and range of
output. On the other hand, production for other people's
consumption or use—especially where production is on a large

scale, and notably where distribution is made a matter of public service or dealt with by the Consumers' Co-operative Movement—has plainly given more food per head, vastly more clothing per family, and a perfectly enormous increase in the variety and range of commodities and services accessible to the whole population. The amateur home-producer who takes to producing for wages, and to buying with his wages what his family requires, finds that he gets more commodities, and has his leisure set free! This, in the last analysis, is why clothes, even the simplest, are no longer made at home, even by the poorest; and why, accordingly, the Clothing Trades have developed, and are developing, in the way that this useful little book describes.

PASSFIELD CORNER,
    LIPHOOK, HANTS,
        August 1928.

The Clothing Workers of Great Britain

CHAPTER I

INTRODUCTORY

" IN 1830 tailors made all the clothing that was worn, save only the makeshifts made by the housewives of the agricultural labourer. It is less than one hundred years ago that a female tailor was unknown, when a sewing-machine was never used in making tailoring, when outworkers were unnecessary. . . . In 1850 a pawnbroker's assistant employed the first Jew and the first sewing-machine in Leeds to make clothing. He had scarcely any money ; if he had made a score of suits he pawned them until he could sell them from a sample and get the money. The firm that he built up can now make 2000 suits per day." [1] The industry that has sprung from these small beginnings now employs over half a million people in this country on the manufacturing side alone, not to mention the vast host of clerical workers, salesmen, travellers, editors of trade newspapers and others essential to the conduct of a great modern industry. It stands to-day in a particularly interesting position, embracing as it does every variety of industrial organization, from the single man or woman plying a needle for the retail customer to the factory employing several thousand hands, equipped with complicated electrically driven machinery, where production is carried on by means of a

[1] Address by Mr B. W. Poole reported in *The Sartorial Gazette* (March 1924).

A

minute subdivision of operations. In some of these factories as many as seventy different operatives handle one lounge coat in the course of its production. In between these extremes we can see clothes being made by hand in the worker's home for a middleman, clothes being made under the same circumstances by machines driven in most cases by power, clothes being made in small workshops either to order or for the wholesale trade, clothes being made for sale to a customer in the next street, and clothes being made for export to Australia or South Africa. Thus the clothing industry, like that much smaller group of trades, the cutlery industry, is still in a state of transition, though this transition seems now to be reaching its final stages.

Long after the introduction of the spinning-jenny and the power-loom had revolutionized the textile trades, clothes were being made after the immemorial methods of our ancestors. A glimpse of these methods—the methods that were still universal at the time when the pawnbroker's assistant started out on his modest experiment in Leeds—is afforded by the following extract from a speech delivered in 1925 by a member of the National Federation of Merchant Tailors. " My earliest sartorial recollection extends back to the time when I was quite a small boy, and spent twelve months under the charge of my grandfather in the country. One indelible incident was the advent of the tailor into the house with his goose, sleeve-board and other impedimenta of the working tailor's craft. He set up his workshop in the ' parlour ' of the farmhouse and there plied his needle until he had satisfied the needs of the family. He made a suit for me, and did some repairs, which I know received anything but commendation from my mother when I returned home. They were strong and well-sewn, but probably lacked style. As soon as Mr Snip had reclothed all the family he went on to the next farm. ' Whipping the cat ' is a thing of the past now. With it have also gone the woollen houses who used to supply the material direct to the customer, who either took it to be made up to a small working tailor or kept it in the house until the arrival of the travelling workman." It need hardly be added that garments requiring less skill, such as shirts and underclothes, were at this date all made at home.

Developments after the middle of the nineteenth century were rapid, and within forty years the wholesale trade was well established for the manufacture of the common sort of men's clothing. At first there were few repercussions on the welfare of the old handicraft tailor. The new industry rather had the effect of providing for a new market. The workman who had hitherto been content to pass his life in corduroy or moleskin now took to buying a new suit of tweeds " off the peg " once a year or oftener. The new suit was, to start with, only worn on Sundays, but soon it came into everyday wear, until to-day corduroy has been relegated to the use of navvies and tramps.

Side by side with the factories there was growing up that army of underpaid, overworked men, women and children, whose existence came with such a shock to the pioneer reformers of the 'eighties, when the " sweating " problem was first heard of. Sweated workers were engaged in a great variety of occupations, but chief among them was the manufacture of clothing, from coronation robes and court dresses to cheap cotton shirts for export to African negroes and Chinese coolies. In some cases the clothing made by the sweated workers competed with or supplemented that made in the factories, in other cases it was sold to working-class families who would otherwise have made their own.

For some twenty years further changes in the industry were few. New factories were gradually being built or old factories adapted for the manufacture of ready-made suits ; the army of the sweated grew larger and more underpaid ; while the handicraft tailor still sat at his bench with his legs crossed and his pipe alight, breathing an unhealthy atmosphere and straining his eyes in an uncertain light, earning "big money" for a few months and almost unemployed for half the year, but working day and night in the "season"; miserably depressed at times, but fond of his work and his companions, and on the whole astonishingly light-hearted. In every village, too, and country town and large city, there remained the thousands of private dressmakers, perhaps employing a few girls to help them, and catering for the needs of women and children.

In the past fifteen years all this has changed. The Trade Board Act of 1909 and the more far-reaching Act of 1918 have improved the lot of the home-worker and indirectly helped to drive many home-workers into the factory and many dressmakers out of business.[1] The restriction of immigration has cut off the supply of trained Jewish workers, while the growing disinclination shown by tailors' sons to follow in their fathers' footsteps has had the same effect on English labour, and thus made it increasingly difficult to obtain "handicraft" tailoring of the old standard of excellence. Meanwhile technical improvements in machinery and the invention of machines for new operations have made vast differences in the quality of the factory-made suit, and women's garments are now for the first time being made in bulk by factory methods. Very soon it seems as if only the most exclusive of men's and women's clothes will be made by hand, so that dressmaking and handicraft tailoring will become purely luxury trades. With this change has appeared a considerable degree of increased standardization in wages, hours of work and conditions, partly as a result of the Trade Board Acts and partly as the result of improved organization both among employers and employed. The time is perhaps not far distant when clothing will take its place beside textiles, engineering, shipbuilding, and the

[1] See Dorothy Sells, *The British Trade Board System.*

other staple trades of the country, in which nation-wide organization accompanies a considerable degree of uniformity of methods and conditions.

And yet, at the present moment, the variety we are faced with is still sufficiently bewildering. Wages, it is true, in so far as the Trade Board regulations are adequately enforced, have been levelled up, and so, to some extent, have conditions inside the factories, though there is a world of difference between an establishment in which the bare requirements of Government and Local Authority Inspectors are reluctantly met, and one where every turn reveals to the stranger with what solicitude the employer has studied the welfare of his staff— a type of establishment which, though rare, is occasionally to be encountered. Again, the basic process, sewing by power-driven machinery, except, of course, in handicraft tailoring, is everywhere the same. But in other matters there is no standardization to be found. The number of employees in a factory or workshop may vary from 5 to 5000 ; the market catered for may lie within a few miles' radius or may extend to the confines of the globe. Even if the clothing manufacturer is normally a man of moderate substance, sober and industrious, conservative and inclined to be narrow-minded, well fitted for the immediate task but lacking vision, he may also be a brilliant and rather unscrupulous financier, or merely a block-head who has inherited his position, or a man who started from humble beginnings and is gradually building up a little business of his own, largely perhaps on borrowed capital ; or again, the value of the property may run into hundreds of thousands and the ownership be vested in an army of share-holders.

As in the more spectacular industries, such as steel or oil or chemicals, the phenomena of vertical and horizontal integration are to be found in endless variety. The normal arrangement is for the material to be bought and made into clothes by the clothing manufacturer and for the completed garments to be sold by him, either direct to the retailer, or more commonly to a wholesale house, for ultimate distribution to the public. But this is by no means universal. Sometimes the wholesale clothier will maintain his own retail shops ; sometimes, but more rarely, he will manufacture at least half of his own cloth, or at any rate have a controlling interest in a cloth firm ; or he may do both these things. On the other hand, we find cases where not even the whole process of turning cloth into clothes is done by one establishment. There is the " cut, make and trim " firm, which only makes up the materials supplied to it by the "clothing manufacturer" and returns them to the latter for disposal, and there is the subcontractor who merely makes up a suit from materials already cut out. Then again, the amount of specialization on particular lines varies enormously. There is the clothing manufacturer who confines himself to artisans' clothing, or to tropical wear, or to railway uniforms. There is the dressmaking firm which will turn out almost any garment of light material for feminine wear, from cotton nightdresses to silk jumpers. There is the merchant-house or the department-store which manufactures clothing of all types, possibly in half a dozen different factories, for sale to its customers, combining these activities with the maufacture, purchase and sale of a hundred other articles. Of these, the Co-operative Wholesale Society, with its clothing factories at Leeds, Manchester, Crewe, Newcastle, London, and Brislington, its shirt factories at Manchester, Sheffield, Newcastle and Cardiff, its mantle and underclothing factories in Manchester, and its corset factories in Desborough and Bristol, is a good example. Finally, a large industrial corporation or a Government department may maintain a clothing factory exclusively for the production of uniforms for its employees ; such is the case with some Railway Companies and the War Office.

This variety in type of employer, and the scale and character

of each firm's output, finds its counterpart in the variety of
personnel employed. Thus in the " sittings " of Soho we shall
find skilled tailors, discontented with their lot, but still maintaining the traditions of their craft, and, on the other side of
Oxford Street, countless busy Jews and Jewesses in subcontractors' workshops, working steadily on less artistic but
more up-to-date lines, and though engaged on a lower class
of trade, earning more money than the handicraftsmen who
despise them as " dirty furriners." We shall find also the
fashionably attired " flappers " in the millinery and dressmaking workshops of famous London houses, and contrast
with them the struggling middle-aged dressmaker in Cornwall,
with nothing to look forward to in her declining years but
declining trade and declining strength, and an old-age pension
in the nearer distance. Going north to Lancashire or the West
Riding, we shall find the sturdy Trade Unionists of Wigan or
of Hebden Bridge, and the efficient, well-paid operatives in
the mammoth factories of Leeds, and perhaps forget that even
now there lies in many a byway of our industrial towns a
tragedy of a widow or a drunkard's wife, striving in ill-health
to maintain a family of young children on the earnings of her
needle in such time as she can spare from the constant round
of household duties.

The purpose of this study is not so much to present an exact
and statistical analysis of the various aspects of the industry
as to give the reader some idea of its multifarious activities,
of the places where it is carried on, and of the people engaged
in it. Statistical data will be sparingly introduced, so far as
available, where they seem to be urgently called for ; but their
compilation, and even their presentation to the public, is
rather the work of a Government department than of an
isolated investigator.

There remains a further point. Many aspects of the clothing
trades have been touched on or treated at length elsewhere ;

as far as possible an attempt will be made not to cover ground which has already been trodden hard by others. With this purpose in view, London, the most important and the most picturesque clothing district of all, has been very summarily dealt with. So much has already been written about the West End tailoring trade, as well as about the innumerable occupations, among which that of the clothing workers takes a prominent place, of the population of East London,[1] that it seems superfluous to write more. It may be added that the task of the investigator in London is perhaps more arduous than it is in other parts of the country. In a town like Leeds it is easy to find out what one wants about the clothing trade without undue delay. The leading factories stare one in the face, the principal factory owners are men who are well-known in the district and easily accessible, the workers are well organized and their Union maintains an efficient office ready to furnish information on request. When a large proportion of a city's population is engaged in a particular industry, it is likely to be an industry about which there are few secrets. In East London all is different. True, there are many clothing workers and many clothing factories. But they are widely dispersed. The average factory is small ; the average employer is a Nobody, in a city where even Somebodies count but little. The workers' organization is weak, and its local officials, though qualified for the discharge of their duties, are comparatively ignorant and incapable of taking a broad view of the industry whose personnel they represent. There is no obliging Chamber of Commerce anxious to display its wares ; no convenient local records exist. Moreover, the area to be covered is almost too large for a single individual to cope with ; lost in a forest of which he can only see the trees, he finds it impossible to formulate in concise language a conception of the entire area.

In Chapter II will be found a brief classification of the

---

[1] See Bibliography on pp. 203-4.

clothing trades as they are organized in this country. This is followed in Chapter III by a survey of the various districts in which they are concentrated, with some consideration of the reasons which have led to their present localization. The rest of the book deals mainly with questions of personnel—the wages earned, the conditions under which work is performed, the organization of employers and employed and the methods whereby new workers are obtained. Some space is devoted to Government regulation of the industry and some consideration is accorded to a comparison between the present and the past. It is thus hoped, not to deal exhaustively with minor points, but rather to draw attention to some of the problems which face one of the country's leading industries.

CHAPTER II

THE CLOTHING TRADES

THOUGH the expression " Clothing Trades " might be logically applied to the manufacture of every article of human apparel or adornment, it is not usually given so wide a scope. The boot and shoe industry forms one important exception, being invariably treated separately. In this enquiry the hosiery and lace trades will also be omitted from consideration. Certain other omissions will be made on grounds of convenience rather than of logic. Amongst these the most important are hats (other than millinery, which is commonly allied to light dressmaking), corsets (except incidentally), and the fur and fancy feather trade. We are thus practically left with all those trades by which textile materials of various kinds are made up into clothes, the most important operation in the process being sewing, either by hand or machine. They are not quite identical with the sewing trades as a whole, since these would include the manufacture of sheets, table-cloths, etc., but they are very nearly so. Sewing in fact is the industrial process which is the least common denominator of the trades we shall consider.

In the evolution of modern industry these trades have fallen into certain well-marked groups, as under :

1. *Tailoring : Retail Bespoke.*

2. *Tailoring : Wholesale*—including (*a*) Men's Wholesale Tailoring—the manufacture of men's and boys' suits, coats and outer clothing generally (Bespoke or Ready-made).

10

(b) The Mantle Trade—the manufacture of women's and girls' costumes, coats, skirts and outer clothing generally of heavy material.

3. *Light Dressmaking*—this usually includes the manufacture of women's underclothing, as well as outer garments of light materials.

4. *Shirts*—including the manufacture of collars, pyjamas, overalls, etc.

We shall now describe these sections in greater detail.

1. RETAIL TAILORING

Before the invention of the sewing-machine, clothes were all either made at home by those who could not afford to have them made by a tailor, or to order for those who could. In those days the journeyman tailor was one of the familiar figures of everyday life. With the gradual improvement of mechanical methods, the handicraft workers' clientèle has steadily dwindled, till to-day they number but a few thousands —perhaps 20,000, probably less, in all Great Britain. A quarter of this number are to be found in the West End of London ; a few hundred in each of the large provincial towns —Birmingham, Sheffield, Bristol, Newcastle-on-Tyne, Nottingham, Portsmouth. The most important towns after London from this point of view are Liverpool, Manchester, Edinburgh and Glasgow. Manchester and Glasgow boast the largest number of workers, while Liverpool and Edinburgh perhaps do the highest class of trade. In smaller country towns there will be perhaps twenty, perhaps thirty, perhaps fifty. Some of the smaller industrial towns of the north still boast a fair number ; so do county towns and cathedral cities ; so do towns where there is a large public school or a well-known hunt near-by ; and especially the University towns of Oxford and Cambridge. Even in the larger villages there are still isolated tailors here and there, though one must now count individuals where one used to count by dozens. The main output of handicraft tailors consists of men's suits and overcoats, especially the former, the latter, owing to the fact that they need not fit exactly, being not infrequently bought ready-made by men who never dream of wearing a ready-made suit. Riding-breeches are perhaps next in importance and require a high degree of skill to ensure a perfect fit. Court and diplomatic uniforms fall into a special category and are only made in London. At one time ladies' tailoring was a flourishing business, but in recent years it has declined in importance, though there is a certain demand for tailor-made coats and skirts, both in London and other centres. For each of these different classes of garments there is a special " log " rate of payment, a highly complicated system of piece-wages.

Ideally, the journeyman tailor makes his garment throughout with his own unaided hands. The cutting is, of course, done by the expert cutter, except in the case of the village tailor, who himself cuts as well as makes. The tailor not only bastes and fells, puts on the collar and does the pressing with the tailors' " goose " as the work progresses, but himself makes the button-holes and sews on the buttons—all without the use of even a hand-driven sewing-machine. This ideal practice, however, is very rarely found to-day. Nearly always he will have at least one woman to help him, and very frequently there will be two. In these cases, the women are responsible for linings, button-holes and buttons, trouser-finishing, sometimes felling, and, generally, all that part of the work which requires comparatively little skill. In London the men-tailors always specialize on one particular kind of garment—thus there are waistcoat hands, coat hands, trouser hands, each of whom makes his own part of the suit. In the case of small country tailors this is not so, but the small country tailor is almost extinct. The coat hand is perhaps the most highly-

skilled of all, and not the least important part of his work—
that which especially distinguishes it from the best type of
factory production—lies in the skill with which he wields the
goose, stretching the material a little here, contracting it
slightly there, and gradually shaping it so that the fit, especially
over the shoulders and round the neck, shall exactly follow the
lines of the human body. Such skill sometimes amounts to
real artistry, and together with the work of the experienced
cutter makes it possible to obtain, say, sixteen guineas for a
suit which without it might fetch seven or eight. But the
handicraft tailor is exceptional ; let us turn to methods which
are to-day more typical in the retail bespoke trade.

All systems of production, in which each garment is entrusted, not to a single man, with or without his female help,
but to a team of workers, may be styled " subdivisional,"
though the exact lines on which the work is arranged are
subject to innumerable variations. One employer will favour
one method ; another, another. There is none of that standardization of processes which is growing increasingly typical
of factory industries, though not, be it said, of the clothing
trades, even when carried on in factories. The question of
what is the ideal subdivisional team is one which has been
much discussed recently in tailoring circles, since it is clear
that some form of subdivision will have to be universally
introduced. There is at present a tendency amongst employers
to treat their own particular method as a trade secret and to
make a mystery of it. This is probably, however, as much due
to a reluctance to confess that any subdivision at all has been
introduced, as to fear that rivals will be able to benefit by a
knowledge of details. Such fear might indeed be justified in
the case of highly elaborate systems of factory organization,
but can scarcely be so where only four or five workers are
employed in a team. Obviously, again, individual circumstances will largely determine the actual system adopted.

It is difficult to say which of the somewhat similar systems would be the best in practice under identical conditions, since conditions in different cases are but rarely identical.

Perhaps the simplest system which could be described as subdivisional is one in which the old handicraft methods still largely predominate. Each garment is entrusted to one man, with two girls to help, but, in addition, to every two or three teams a machinist is provided. Employers who use this system generally prefer not to apply the obnoxious epithet " subdivisional " to it at all. It clearly has considerable merits, combining as it does the chief features of the old handicraft tailoring with the immense saving of time effected by having done by machine the parts of the work where hand-sewing can claim no definite advantage. A little more elaborate would be a team of one skilled tailor, two skilled tailoresses, a machinist and a couple of apprentices. This still provides for a large amount of handwork, though much of it is done by women, who are not considered so capable as men for the difficult parts of the work. Another actual example of a team is one consisting of a foreman, two tailors, two machinists, two finishers, one presser and one girl apprentice. As soon as the tailoring and pressing are done by different people the most characteristic feature of the journeyman tailor's work is lost. Nevertheless, with such a team as the one just described, though much of the work is done by machine, garments of very good quality can be turned out. The four essential processes are : (a) basting (done by the tailors), (b) machining, (c) pressing, (d) finishing (buttons and button-holes). Even larger teams are by no means uncommon in subdivisional workshops —in fact they are perhaps usual, especially in the provinces. In some cases, where each operative concentrates on some small part of the garment, ceaselessly repeating the same process in a mechanical manner, there is nothing to distinguish the workshop from the factory, except the technical distinction that it contains no power-driven machinery.

Unlike handicraft tailoring which is manned by British craftsmen, together with a fair scattering of Swedes and other continental races, the subdivisional trade is almost exclusively in the hands of Jews. It was originally adopted by, and is still most commonly associated with, the Jewish subcontractor who accepts work from the retail tailor at a fixed price per garment, pays his own employees a time-wage and nearly always works himself—at least at the outset of his career. These sub-contractors would usually start as employees and after a while set up in a small way as independent " master-tailors." [1] There has, however, of late years been a tendency for British retail employers to adopt subdivisional methods in their own workshops, sometimes engaging Jewish labour for the purpose, but often introducing British workers to the system. There are also, in many towns in the north, especially Sheffield, a large number of Jewish masters who habitually use subdivi-sional methods in the retail trade. Alongside this tendency for subdivisional methods to spread, there has been a ten-dency for the subcontractor to disappear, and for his place to be taken by the high-class manufacturer. At present this is kept in check by the ever-growing encroachment of the subcontractor on the domain of the handicraft tailor. But the time will soon come when handicraft tailoring will be obsolete, or nearly so, and then we may perhaps see only two methods of making clothes survive —making to measure by subdivisional methods, on the retailer's premises without any subcontracting, and making either "to measure" or "ready-made" in factories, either to the order of the retailer or for stock. It is too soon to dogmatize

---

[1] Not to be confused with high-class retail tailors, who also style themselves " master-tailors," and whose trade organization is styled " The Association of London Master Tailors." The subcontractors' organization is called " The Master Tailors Association."

on this point. Such a consummation is, however, to be welcomed and encouraged. The subcontractor is between the devil and the deep blue sea. Pressed by the retailer and by the competition of his rivals to accept work at constantly lower prices, he has only two alternatives. Either the quality of the work must suffer, so that finally it falls far below the level of the best factory-made clothes, or the workers must be overdriven and underpaid. In the past the worst horrors of sweating have frequently been associated with the subcontractor. This has largely been remedied, though it is still harder to enforce Government regulations amongst the vast army of subcontractors than in factories. Especially is this true of conditions of work. The Jewish employer is not usually the worst offender in the matter of wages. If he gets what he wants he is willing to pay good money for it. But he is apt to neglect questions of ventilation and sanitation, and, a hard worker himself, he gives no quarter to those who do not come up to his own exacting standards in the matter of speed.

Besides working for individual retail shops, subcontractors find an increasing class of customers among firms of the multiple-shop type, such as Curzons, Ltd. Some of these firms make their own clothes in their own factories, but others deal exclusively with subcontractors. A favourite method is for the multiple shop to buy the cloth, and invoice it to the subcontractor, who then makes suits from it as ordered, selling the suit back to the multiple firm at a price which covers what he paid for the cloth, together with a fixed price per suit for cutting and making it. The subcontractor usually supplies the trimmings, lining, buttons, etc., himself. This is known as the " cut, make and trim " trade. In other cases the material is cut by the retailer and merely sent, complete with trimmings, to the subcontractor to be made up. " Cut, make and trim " houses also do work for wholesale clothiers, either when the wholesale manufacturer receives orders of a kind with which he is not prepared to deal himself; orders, for instance, for "bespoke" garments, when he only makes "ready-mades" on the premises, or in times of pressure, when he has more orders than his own staff and plant can cope with. This is very common in Leeds.

2. (a) WHOLESALE TAILORING

There are two sections of the wholesale tailoring trade—the bespoke or "to order" section and the "ready-made" section. Some firms apply themselves exclusively to one or the other of these; more usually, both trades are, to some extent anyway, carried on by the same establishment. A firm which is chiefly engaged in making ready-mades is nearly always prepared to execute "special" orders if required; those with a very low class of trade or working entirely on contracts being the only exceptions. On the other hand, while some manufacturers, particularly some of those owning their own retail stores, profess to make every garment to the customer's special order, they almost invariably fill up slack times by a certain amount of making for stock. A better classification would be according to the kind of market catered for. It is not usual for a firm doing high-class work, requiring a certain amount of hand-tailoring, to combine with this low-grade export orders, or *vice versa*. If a firm doing a high-class trade is asked to supply a type of garment it is not in the habit of making itself, it will not normally refuse the order but will pass it on to a manufacturer able to execute it. This practice is quite common. It is also common for a firm making, say, coats and suits, to purchase, for resale, raincoats for the convenience of their customers. In Leeds, in particular, specialization on the part of wholesale clothiers is highly developed. In one establishment quality of workmanship is considered to be of greater importance than size of output; in another speed is the only goal to be aimed at, and a mistake

B

here and there may perhaps be overlooked. So much is this so that the workers become specialized, and can only obtain fresh employment in the same class of firm as that for which they previously worked. This is not to say that the high-class firms necessarily pay the best wages, any more than the Rolls-Royce Company necessarily pays better than Henry Ford; very often indeed the reverse is the case, though not always. The point is that the special aptitudes required for the different kinds of work are not the same. In less highly organized centres than Leeds specialization is less marked, but it is still present. The chief of these are Manchester, London, Bristol, Glasgow, Plymouth, Kettering, Leicester and Wigan. The firms with a high-class trade usually have a large " special " (*i.e.* bespoke) department. Their chief market is found in the big department stores in the West End and in large provincial towns—firms like Selfridge's, Harrods' and Barkers'. A lower grade of work is done by the firm which makes ready-mades mainly for sale in working-class districts or for export. Many of these firms, as we have seen, have their own retail stores, this practice having grown enormously in recent years. These are principally situated in Leeds and Glasgow. Others sell direct to retailers through their travellers, others again sell largely to dry-goods merchants, who then distribute to retailers at home or in foreign markets. Some merchant-houses have their own factories—for example, Cook, Son & Co., of St. Paul's Churchyard, though this company also makes purchases elsewhere. In a special position is the Co-operative Wholesale Society, which, though not owning its own retail stores, sells exclusively to Consumers' Societies, doing a medium trade in both specials and ready-mades. Other firms have a still lower class of trade, often destined for the Kaffir market.[1] In Hebden Bridge is concentrated the

---

[1] London is the centre for the Kaffir trade; Leeds for the lowest (as well as the highest) class of home trade.

manufacture of cords, moles, fustians, etc.—a class of garment that has gone much out of favour in recent years. Then there are other firms in various centres engaged wholely or chiefly on contract work, of which there is a very large and increasing amount being done for Government and municipal departments and for industrial companies—uniforms for tramwaymen and policemen, for postmen, railwaymen and the naval, military and air forces. The War Office has its own factory— the Royal Army Clothing Factory at Pimlico. So, for instance, has the L.M. and S. Railway at Crewe. It is said that there are close rings among the contract firms to prevent competition in tendering for orders ; undoubtedly a certain amount of mutual understanding prevails. Contract houses are particularly numerous in London and Leeds. Another special line is the manufacture of tropical wear ; this is catered for in Manchester, London and, especially, East Anglia—Norwich and Colchester.

Apart from the regular centres, wholesale clothiers, especially those which cater for low-grade markets, are to be found in various country districts, where the low wages prevalent among agricultural workers, and the lack of employment for women, provide a large and cheap female labour market, a factor which offsets the disadvantages of an isolated situation. This is particularly true of the South of England ; Basingstoke, for instance, has a small clothing industry, depending for its labour force not merely on the town itself but on the surrounding district.

With regard to the methods of work, what has been said of the retail subdivisional trade is also true of the wholesale trade—there is very little standardization. The main lines on which the work is arranged are, it is true, dictated by the nature of the machinery employed, but individual manufacturers are free to pursue their own ideas within wide limits. The contrast between any old-fashioned firm and one recently established, in regard to general layout and to the proportion of machinery employed, is often very remarkable. The machinery is made by a comparatively small number of firms, of which Singers is the best known. Every year sees some new device being introduced, special machines for button-holing, for instance; or for sewing on buttons. The Hoffman press, too, has been adapted in various ways for various special purposes, so that, while one firm will use a limited number of different types of machines, and a type of press that can be put to different purposes, another and more up-to-date one will install every new device as it is put on the market, and consequently will have to adopt a far more minute specialization of processes. To some extent the possibility of doing this will of course depend on the size of the firm, some machines being a source of unnecessary expense unless the output is so large that they can be kept in constant employment. At the same time it is not by any means always the largest firms which have the highest degree of specialization.

The following is a typical set of processes for the construction of a coat in an up-to-date factory, which yet stops short of the minute specialization more common in America than in this country. The first processes are the entering of the order in a ledger and the cutting off of the requisite length of cloth. The next process is the cutting. If the order is for a large number of identical garments, the cutting is done by means of a band-knife, which will cut up to 60 thicknesses. If it is for a single coat, an ordinary pair of cutter's shears is used. In both cases the cutting is nearly always done by men. For stock sizes a perforated lay is placed on the cloth and sprinkled with powdered chalk. On removal of the lay, the pattern will be marked out in chalk on the material. In other cases the nearest available pattern will be used, and the cutter will make the necessary variations from it; this requires a high degree of skill and long experience. Next the necessary trimmings (*i.e.* linings, etc.) must be cut. As the material here is of less value, and a certain overlap is permissible, the trimmer, who is usually a boy or a woman, requires far less skill than the cutter. The cloth and trimmings are then passed to the "fitter-up," who is usually a man employed on time-wages, but may occasionally be a woman. Very often the fitter-up is the foreman or the forewoman of one room or section of a room in the factory. Most wholesale clothiers dislike employing forewomen, even though the machinists under them are all girls. They say that women are more addicted to favouritism than are men. Others are less exacting, but usually there is a male foreman in charge of the room, even where forewomen are working beneath him.[1] The work next goes to the machinist —a woman, employed (except for a few odd hands, such as alteration hands) on piece-wages. As a general rule, we may add, all work which admits of it is paid for by the piece. Some of the finishers may have to be paid time-wages, and pressing is sometimes paid by "time" and sometimes by "piece." It is in the machining that perhaps the greatest variety of processes is to be found. After the seams have been machined, the garment, as we may now call it, goes to the seam-presser, then to the bridler, who fixes the collar, which has meantime been made by another hand. Next a young girl puts in the padding. All these processes however, except the seam-pressing, may be done by one worker. Next the under-presser —a man—shapes the collar, then returns the coat to the machinist, who fixes the collar to the lining and sends it back to the presser. After the presser has done his work, the coat, which has so far been inside out, goes to the "liner-in," who "bags" it "out." Thence it passes to the "edge-baster"

[1] In the mantle trade, in which the conditions of work are substantially similar, forewomen are the general rule. Thus the objection to them in wholesale clothing is partly to be attributed to prejudice· In dressmaking there is often not a single male employee, though sometimes cutters and designers are men.

(who bastes the edges), the "edge-presser"—a girl (who presses the edges), and then to the "edge-stitcher" (who stitches them). Then it goes on to the sleeving-machinist, where the sleeves, previously made by the machinist, are sewn on by a special machine, to the button-holer (who may work by hand or machine) and the finisher, who fells the bottom of the coat and does any other finishing that has not been done elsewhere. After a final pressing it passes to the "button-marker" and "buttoner," whose names indicate their occupations, and finally to the "passer," generally a man, who inspects the garment. If it is satisfactory it is sent off to the dispatch-room. Thus there are at least a dozen different pairs of hands through which the coat must go. Often there are far more. Trousers are more easily made, being machined throughout by the same person, passed on to the button-holer, thence to the seam-presser, and so to the buttoner, who in this case nearly always does the work by machine. Waistcoats go through a somewhat similar though rather simpler process than coats.

The arrangement of rooms inside a factory varies enormously with the size of the firm, the date at which the premises were built, and according as they were originally erected as a clothing factory, or have since been adapted to the purpose for which they are now used. As the machinery required is easily installed into any existing premises, the latter state of affairs is by no means uncommon, especially, as might be expected, in the case of small establishments in towns. In a typical factory in Leeds, besides the offices, employees' rest- and dining-rooms, etc., there is the woollen-room, where cloth is stored, the cutting-room, a machine-room for coats, another for vests, another for trousers, a finishing-room and a passing-room ; as well as a separate department for the making of specials. This is a firm with some 300 employees. In another case a firm with about 4000 employees has, apart from the offices, etc., and the woollen-room, only two gigantic rooms, both on the ground floor, with overhead lighting, one the cutting-room, and the other the machine-room. Most of the better firms have good accommodation for the employees' meals, and good conditions generally. On the other hand some small establishments are cramped and unsuitable. Wages are usually well up to Trade Board standards ; the chief abuse occurs when outworkers are employed in rush-periods, or, as still sometimes prevails in some centres, continuously for trouser finishing. In these cases, the outworkers frequently connive at a breach of the regulations by waiting on the premises for work without being paid for their " waiting-time." This is an evil it is difficult to eradicate. The practice of " dead-horse " used to be common but is now seldom found. This was the habit of paying the piece-worker a minimum weekly wage, even when there is not enough work to allow of this wage being earned at the existing piece-rates, and keeping a record of the excess thus paid. The employee is then regarded as owing so much work to the firm, and in busy times is compelled to do it without receiving any payment. Before the Trade Board regulations this was a lawful practice, though objectionable if carried at all far. Where a minimum time-wage has to be paid, it is of course illegal.

It has been seen that, with the exception of cutters, pressers and foremen, all the employees are women. Usually Jewish labour is to be found when the employer is a Jew. This is not, however, an invariable rule. In most factories owned by Gentiles, it is usual, if Jews are employed, to provide one room for Jews and one for Gentiles, the view being taken that the two races will not mix. On the other hand there are cases where no distinction is made. Even where Jewish men are objected to, Jewish women seem to be less unpopular ; some old-fashioned employers, however, have a rooted antipathy to employing either the men or the women—at least on their own premises. These same manufacturers very frequently, however, have their best work done by Jewish subcontractors, only entrusting the lower grade to Christian hands! The general tendency, especially in Leeds, where Jewish labour in factories is commonest, is for the race-distinction to disappear.

2. (b) THE MANTLE TRADE

Whilst in the retail section men's and women's tailoring may be regarded as part of a single trade, though individual tailors may specialize on one or the other, in the wholesale there is a clear distinction between " Clothing," which in this connotation means men's outer garments, and " Mantles," which means women's outer garments. Only in rare cases will the same firm engage in the manufacture of both men's and women's clothes. A meeting-point for the two trades is provided by the Juvenile section, little boys' suits being frequently made by mantle firms as well as by wholesale clothiers.

The general organization of the mantle and clothing trades is naturally very similar, but there are one or two important points of difference which it is worth while noting. To begin with, there is the question of design. In the men's trade fashions change but slowly, and designing accordingly occupies a place of secondary importance. In the women's trade they change with bewildering rapidity and the designer is the most important person in the whole organization. Besides introducing new styles on his own initiative, he must keep in constant touch with changes in fashion in the various centres, particularly in Paris. There exist special firms who publish books of new designs for sale to the trade, and by combining what he can pick up from these with his own ideas, the expert designer will get the best results.

Another effect of the constant changing of fashions is that bulk orders figure far less prominently in the mantle than in the clothing trade. There are, of course, a few stock-lines which are constantly required, *e.g.* "gym-slips," but in the case of ordinary costumes and dresses there is no scope for making in bulk. Apart from changing fashions almost every separate garment must have some slight individuality. Perhaps it is merely that two costumes of exactly the same pattern and material are trimmed a little differently, or the trimming and pattern may be the same and the material of a different shade —and so on. Yet another aspect in which the two trades differ is that, broadly speaking, the materials used in the mantle trade are lighter than in the case of men's clothing, and accordingly a slightly different type of machine and a worker with a different type of skill is required. There is also less scope for elaborate subdivision of processes. It is seldom that a garment passes through more than half a dozen hands in the process of manufacture. Finally, the mantle trade differs from the men's trade, in that an even larger proportion of women is employed—though normally the foremen, pressers and cutters are men.

The most important centre of the trade is Leeds, and next come London and Manchester. Leicester is a bad fourth, and Glasgow is important, but rather as a distributing than a manufacturing centre. Stroud, Bristol, Bath and the surrounding districts used to form another centre, the work being mostly collected and executed by Jewish subcontractors. At the present time, however, the trade has almost, though not quite, deserted the south-west. Birmingham still has a factory employing about 400 hands, and some other large towns— Nottingham for instance—are in a similar position. None the less, Leeds, Manchester and London are the centres which really count.

As regards conditions of work, little need be said, since they are substantially similar to those in the wholesale clothing trade. "Sweating" in its old sense has practically disappeared, though some homework still prevails, particularly in London, and evasion of Trade Board rates is probably not unknown. The usual wage-rates are about the same as those in the men's trade, but, as there are separate Trade Boards for the two trades, they are not always identical. On the whole, perhaps, they are slightly lower. The employees are weakly organized, and special agreements for the payment of wages above the Trade Board rates are rare.

The trade is slightly less subject to seasonal fluctuations than men's clothing, but has of late years become very dependent on the ebb and flow of fashions. It is not suggested that these have become more capricious than of yore, but rather that whereas in the past a change of fashion meant that the mantle industry gave up making one style of garment and started making another, it often means nowadays that the trade languishes altogether while some other branch of the clothing industry prospers exceedingly. At one moment, for instance, there will occur a sudden increase in the demand for knitted costumes, or for skirts and jumpers, none of which garments, with the possible exception of skirts, the mantle trade is equipped to make. This will involve a corresponding fall in the sale of ready-made costumes. At another moment tailor-made coats and skirts may go out of fashion, and the mantle trade reaps the benefit. Both these events have occurred in recent years. In general, however, it may be said, that the mantle trade has been enjoying considerable prosperity, owing to the ever-widening market for ready-made women's clothing.

This expansion is not likely to go very much farther, as practically everybody now purchases mantles and costumes from ladies' outfitters of various types, the old-fashioned dressmaker working for private customers being almost a figure of the past. In some cases customers want their clothes made to measure, but even then they are usually satisfied with wholesale bespoke garments, the annual output of which increases yearly ; the highest class of trade is done by fashionable West End costumiers, who employ highly skilled hands in their own workrooms.

3. LIGHT DRESSMAKING, UNDERCLOTHING AND BABY-LINEN

The chief centre of this trade is London, with nearly 50,000 employees, after which comes Manchester, with 7000. Exact figures are hard to come at, since the census returns under the head of " Dresses and Blouses " include millinery, while underclothing is classed with " Shirts, Collars, Handkerchiefs and Ties," but the above is probably a fairly accurate approximation. It must not be forgotten that the trade is largely a retail one carried on in the workshops of large department stores and even comparatively small drapers' shops, as well as by numberless individuals working on their own.[1] Of the 50,000 workers in London, for instance, less than half are employed by firms in the wholesale trade, while even in Manchester the proportion of factory workers is scarcely more than two in three. It may safely be said that in every town with a population of 200,000 or more there are at least 1000 dressmakers employed by retailers or private customers.

After London and Manchester the most important factory centres are Nottingham, Cardiff, Birmingham, Glasgow, Leeds and Liverpool. Less important are Bristol, Bradford, Halifax and Northampton.

In this trade the number of men employed is quite insignificant. The materials are light and easily handled, so that the cutting as well as all the other processes can be performed by women. Pressers are rarely required, since in most cases the finished garment merely has to be ironed before it is folded and packed. The number of processes into which

[1] To a much smaller extent this is also true of the mantle trade.

the work is divided is not so large as in the heavier trades. A typical scheme is the following, which prevails in a Manchester factory. First comes the cutting, nearly always in bulk with a band-knife adapted to light materials. Next in order comes the making of any trimmings that may be necessary, though these are frequently obtained ready-made from elsewhere. Lace, for instance, at one time far more popular than it is to-day, comes chiefly from Nottingham, while a large quantity of embroidery is imported from Switzerland. Then the various pieces are collected and given to the machinist, who makes the garment throughout. Subdivision at this stage, which, on a limited scale, is common in the making of men's shirts, is almost impossible in the case of women's underclothing, owing to the immense variety and constant minor changes in fashions, which would upset any system of subdivision almost as soon as it had been worked out. Accordingly girls who, if they were employed in the men's trade, would spend the whole of their working lives at one single process, say fixing in linings or machining seams, are here trained to make a garment throughout. This has the triple advantage that the work is far less monotonous, that when out of employment a girl will find it a good deal easier to find a new position to suit her, and that if she gets married, or for any other reason gives up working, she will be well equipped to make the family clothes at home. The machining finished, the garment now passes in succession to the button-hand, the buttoner and the ironer, after which it is ready for the passer, who examines it, and then for the packing department.

The average size of a firm is considerably smaller than is usual in the mantle or wholesale clothing trades. Normally the number of employees is from 40 to 200. It is by no means infrequent to find that the business has been built up from small beginnings by a woman who started out as a private dressmaker. One of the best-known firms in Halifax grew up in this way. Joint-stock companies, comparatively rare in all branches of the clothing trades, are here almost unknown.

Manufacturers of underclothing of the old type, flannel in winter and calicoes and cambrics in summer, have been very severely hit in recent years by the competition of woven artificial silk goods. These are usually made up by special firms employing almost unskilled girls on semi-automatic machinery. The material is supplied by the manufacturers in a cylindrical shape like an endless tube, from which suitable lengths are cut off and " overlocked " at each end by the machines. The garment then requires little more than a pair of ribbon shoulder-straps and perhaps a little trimming to render it ready for wear. In addition to this competition the underclothing firms have to face the fact that the demand for their products has been considerably curtailed by the present tendency to reduce the amount of underclothing worn to a minimum, for reasons of comfort and health. It is probable that fewer women make their underclothes at home than in the past, but the compensation provided by this circumstance is certainly small compared with the loss of trade from other causes.

The foregoing relates principally to the cheap and medium trades. The most expensive underclothes are not usually made in factories but emanate either from abroad—and in particular from France—or from the workrooms of high-class retail shops. This retail trade is in a flourishing condition. Wages are good and there is much competition among girls of about fourteen to enter the trade. Still more is this true of the blouse and light dressmaking sections, where skill and taste are all-important factors. Only specially selected girls are taken on. They have to serve an apprenticeship at a very low wage for the first few years, after which they are in a position to earn good money. These girls come from a higher social class than do most clothing-workers, being generally the daughters of clerical workers or of highly-skilled artisans.

Wages and conditions in the factories are not unlike those in the mantle trade. Here again there is a separate Trade Board, so that some divergence is likely, but not much. Owing to the delicate nature of many of the materials used, it is essential that the factory or workshop should be clean and airy, this being specially true of " white goods." Seasonal fluctuations are not severe. There is, of course, a separate summer and winter trade, but the demand for all, except the heaviest winter clothes, is far more continuous than it is for outer garments.

4. SHIRTS, COLLARS AND PYJAMAS

The most important centre of the shirt trade in the British Isles is Londonderry in Northern Ireland, and thus lies outside the scope of this study, although a large proportion of the leading Derry factories are owned by firms which have a branch in London, Manchester, Glasgow (or rather Paisley) or elsewhere in Great Britain. The three towns just mentioned account for the largest number of workers in the shirt trade on this side of the Irish Sea, while various towns in the south-west of England, headed by Taunton, form a fourth district of importance. In London (especially in Southwark) the number employed is ten or twelve thousand, in Manchester (and Stockport) six thousand, in Glasgow slightly fewer, and in the south-west about four thousand, of whom about half are in Taunton. There are a few shirt factories elsewhere, as at Carlisle and Reading, while in every large town there is a very small retail trade making shirts to the customer's individual order, although the great bulk of the business is in the factory-made article.

The most notable features of recent years in the industry

have been the virtual disappearance of other materials in favour of cotton and the long-continued depression in nearly all lines. At one time linen was largely demanded for summer wear and flannel for the winter. Except for dress shirts, white linen shirts and collars are not now often seen. When they are worn, indeed, it is more likely than not that the so-called linen is really only cotton with a " linen finish." The article now most commonly worn is the " tunic shirt," which is sold either with or without a collar to match. These shirts were originally made in Londonderry, but were introduced into Manchester and other towns some twenty years ago. During the war, the demand for khaki shirts was of course enormous, and after the war was over men returning to civilian life almost all adopted a shirt of the type to which they had grown accustomed in the army, namely a " tunic " shirt worn with a soft collar.

The stagnation in trade is mainly attributable to the loss of export markets both on the continent and overseas. In particular, firms making cheap working-class shirts and " kaffir " goods have suffered from this cause. It is also asserted by manufacturers that the unusually poor weather conditions which have prevailed in recent summers have curtailed the demand for cricket and tennis shirts, though it is difficult to believe that this would be a serious factor over a term of years. Probably a further explanation is afforded by the fact that there was a big war-time expansion in the industry and a great extension in the use of power-driven machinery, which has equipped manufacturers to turn out a vastly increased output.

It was in the shirt trade above all others that the " sweating problem " of pre-war days assumed the most formidable proportions. In the anti-sweating literature of the *Daily News* Exhibition period (*i.e.* 1906–1908), appalling examples of low wages were constantly being brought to light, especially among the outworkers of East London. By the year 1914 matters had substantially improved, no doubt in consequence of the establishment in 1911 of the Shirt Trade Board. The war, however, saw a recrudescence of the evil, particularly in Manchester, where enormous quantities of army shirts were sent out to be made or finished by home-workers. Since the end of the war there is no reasonable doubt that anything that could be described as " sweating " has ceased, chiefly, perhaps, because the existing factories can more than produce the output demanded without having recourse to the home-worker. The only exception is that the very cheapest class of goods, for which, however, the demand has enormously diminished, are still made out at rates which indeed compare favourably with those which used to be paid, but which, it may be suspected, do not always reach the minimum Trade Board standard.

Shirt firms usually make pyjamas also, the materials and processes being very similar. Some also make collars of all kinds, whilst others merely make collars to match the shirts, when they are required. In the case of factories engaged in the cheaper end of the trade, dungarees and overalls are generally turned out as well, again because of the similarity of materials and processes required.

The methods of work are not by any means standardized. In some factories there is a fair amount of subdivision of processes, in others scarcely any, though the cutting, machining and finishing are, as everywhere, in separate hands. On the whole, too much specialization is regarded with disfavour by employers and work-people alike. Conditions of work are also apt to vary a good deal. While some premises are clean, well ventilated and generally speaking up-to-date, others leave much to be desired. The fact that there are a great many comparatively small firms, and that it is possible to adapt old premises with ease, makes this likely. Wages are normally in accordance with minimum Trade Board rates.

CHAPTER III

THE LOCALISATION OF THE INDUSTRY

EVEN to-day there is scarcely a town or village in Great Britain in which the clothing industry in one or other of its many branches is not carried on. But leaving on one side the thousands of little dressmakers' and tailors' establishments which survive at every point, and a few isolated factories to be found in unexpected corners up and down the country, we can distinguish certain clearly defined centres of the industry, each with its own special characteristics. To a large extent, as might be expected, their distribution corresponds with the distribution of the population at large ; but while some very populous districts, such as Birmingham and South Wales, have a clothing industry of but modest dimensions, others, such as Leeds, have what appears to be more than their fair share. The factors at the back of this distribution will, it is hoped, emerge from what follows, as the different districts are discussed in turn. The most important of such factors would appear to be the following : First comes the one already mentioned, namely the distribution of the general population. Since every one must wear clothes, and since we all wear more or less the same clothes, the size of the market in a particular district will vary with the number of people living in it. Moreover, other things being equal (to use what is nowadays rather a dangerous expression), it is natural for an industry to be situated in proximity to its largest market. Next comes the question of raw materials. The principal raw materials of the clothing trades are textile fabrics of wool or cotton, though knitted garments and artificial silk are growing increasingly

C

popular. It is therefore in the great textile districts of Lancashire and the West Riding that one would look for clothing firms, and it is here that one finds them in greatest profusion, especially in the metropolitan towns of Leeds and Manchester, drawing their materials from, and largely, though by no means exclusively, finding their markets in the surrounding towns and rural districts. A third factor which will sometimes account for the existence of a clothing firm where on other grounds one would least expect it, is the presence of an abundant labour market. This may explain why the industry is established in Wellingborough, and in many places in the Southern and Eastern counties, as we shall see in due course. In East London, too, one important advantage enjoyed by the clothing manufacturer is the enormous supply of cheap semi-skilled female labour. Yet another cause may be the fact that a place may be favourably situated for the export trade. This may be the case to some extent with Bristol, which, at one time at least, did a flourishing trade overseas. Lastly, any or all of these factors may have had influence in the past and have now disappeared, in which case historical reasons may be said to be at work, for naturally a trade once established in a place is not likely suddenly to leave it, merely because the causes which originally brought it into being have ceased to operate. This can perhaps best be illustrated by the clothing firms to be found in what was once the great cloth district of the south-west. It must not, of course, be forgotten that in the industrial world chance always plays a dominating part, and that in assigning causes to industrial phenomena we are treading on dangerous ground. The student must be prepared to make broad generalizations, when he is led to them by what he has observed, but he must beware of jumping to conclusions which the facts do not justify.

The principal clothing centres are, then, as follows : At the head of the list we may place Leeds, not because it contains the largest number of clothing operatives, nor because the clothing trades carried on within its boundaries exhibit the greatest diversity of character and method, but because it is the only large town of which it may almost be said that clothing is its staple industry, in the sense in which jute is the staple industry of Dundee or shipping of Liverpool. Indeed, even in Leeds many would assign the premier place to the woollen trades, while engineering of various kinds runs these two a close third. A second district is formed by the neighbouring West Riding towns of Halifax and Huddersfield, especially the former, with which we may include Hebden Bridge and the adjoining villages, the centre of the manufacture of cords and moles. Crossing the Lancashire border, we come to Manchester and its ring of satellite towns. While Leeds specializes in outer garments of which wool is the chief material, Manchester, where cotton reigns supreme, is principally engaged in making dresses of light materials as well as shirts and underclothes. Manchester is also noted for the raincoat industry, which has developed during fairly recent years. The adjoining borough of Stockport makes cloth caps, and the outlying town of Wigan has a few excellent wholesale tailoring firms. Our fourth district is a more scattered one and comprises several towns in the West Midlands, among which Birmingham, Walsall and Newcastle-under-Lyme, are the most noteworthy. The clothing trades here carried on are of a miscellaneous character. Continuing southward we come, in the fifth place, to the district of which Bristol is the centre, and which includes Gloucester and the Stroud valley on the north, and Taunton, Bridgewater and Plymouth on the south. The South Wales towns are sufficiently distinct from the last district to be placed in a separate group of their own, though they only support a small number of clothing workers. In the East Midlands the lace and hosiery centres of Nottingham, Kettering and Leicester are turning their attention to various sewing trades as the older industries decline in importance, and form the seventh group. The eighth district is the Eastern Counties, especially Colchester and Norwich, the leading centres for tropical wear. Finally, if we omit the various towns in the South of England where clothing of one sort or another is made, among them being Portsmouth, Basingstoke and Reading, with several others, on the ground that they are too scattered and unimportant to be described as a " clothing district," we have London. In Greater London the number of clothing workers is round about 150,000. Besides the unique body of handicraft tailors in Soho, this includes representatives of nearly every branch of the trade to be found elsewhere, together with not a few special branches which are peculiar to itself. Jew and Gentile, skilled and unskilled, factory operative and home-worker, tailor and seamstress and milliner, here they all are, and yet in their endless variety they constitute but a single element in the many-sided life of the city, and but a small fraction of its teeming millions.[1]

This completes the list for England. In Scotland there is only one important clothing centre, and that is Glasgow, which is engaged in the wholesale tailoring trade along the lines on which it is pursued in Leeds, but on a much smaller scale. The shirt and collar trade it also shares with London and Manchester, as with Northern Ireland. A few mantles are made, and there is a dressmaking and millinery industry of some magnitude. Edinburgh is famous for its handicraft tailoring, ranking in reputation next after the West End ; otherwise it has no clothing trade to speak of. Ireland is outside our purview.

---

[1] The north-east coast, more especially Newcastle, being a thickly-populated industrial district, can provide a certain number of clothing workers for the Census figures. But since clothing is almost the least important of its many industries, it has not seemed advisable to treat it as a " clothing centre."

While the foregoing list includes all the leading centres, it must be repeated that it is not by any means exhaustive. Ninety per cent., or more, it is true, of the clothing operatives in the country are to be found in one or other of the places named. But there is a considerable retail tailoring trade in every large town, though the advent of the Multiple-Shop clothiers and of the big department stores, which sell garments of all but the highest quality ready-made, has done much to reduce its prosperity. Hull, for instance, which since it contains no clothing factories we have not mentioned, is noteworthy for the number of Jewish subcontractors working exclusively for the local retail trade—and incidentally for the poor conditions prevailing in the workshops. Again, it is not unusual to find in a town otherwise destitute of clothing factories a single establishment catering perhaps for some special local need. Such, for instance, is the Co-operative Wholesale Society's shirt factory in Sheffield, which is principally engaged in turning out rough shirts and dungarees for the steel-workers and engineers, who form the most important section of this town's industrial population. Finally, we must not forget that a large but incalculable proportion of the nation's clothes is made at home by innumerable housewives, ladies' maids and hired dressmakers, as well as in institutions of a religious, charitable, or reformatory character.

We may now proceed to study the characteristics of the foregoing groups in greater detail.

LEEDS

Out of a total population of 450,000, perhaps 35,000 (of whom, say, 5000 are Jews), are engaged in Leeds in one or the other of the clothing trades. Of these the great majority —over 31,000—are classed by the Census as being engaged in " tailoring," which means for the most part, the wholesale men's and boys' clothing trades, though it, of course, includes any one employed in the retail trade, as well as a number of operatives in mantle factories. The staple material in the case of " tailoring " is woollen cloth. Thus if we exclude an isolated shirt factory here, a blouse or raincoat factory there, the trade is from one point of view very homogeneous. But from another point of view it presents a picture of infinite diversity. The total number of clothing firms within the boundaries of the town is from three to four thousand, differing widely in size, in structure, in methods of work and in the efficiency with which they are managed.

In the forefront loom half a dozen gigantic factories employing a thousand or more, and in at least two cases some 3000 or 4000 hands. Each of these large firms has its own peculiar characteristics. There is, for instance, the venerable establishment of John Barran & Co., which claims to be the pioneer of the wholesale clothing trade. The original founder started in business with a few employees some eighty years ago, when the sewing-machine was in its infancy. As might be expected, this firm, which is now a limited company with a registered capital of £510,000, pursues a very conservative policy. The bulk of its trade is in high-grade ready-mades, but there is also a rapidly developing bespoke department. At one time an attempt was made to cater for the American market ; after a few years this policy was abandoned and the firm has returned to the plan of maintaining and strengthening its home connections. The experience of this firm has been shared by many others which have attempted to cultivate a foreign market. Different countries nearly always show slight differences in the style of clothes they favour. Though this is less noticeable in regard to men's than to women's clothes, it is usually sufficient to prevent the development of any very large export trade, except, of course, in the lowest class of clothes, such as " Kafir " goods, which will always be bought in the cheapest

market. In the case of Barrans' American trade, it was hoped
that the traditional excellence of British-tailored clothes
would carry the day, especially in an Anglo-Saxon country.
As it turned out, while there is no doubt that wealthy Americans
come to England to have their clothes made, the type of man
who wants clothes not made to measure, but the very best
quality of ready-mades, is quite prepared to accept the products
of American firms. No doubt the high American tariff on
imported manufactures also helped to stifle the trade where
it showed any signs of development. When the war broke
out, with its attendant inconveniences for the foreign trader,
the weakling infant died a natural death. The only countries,
indeed, where British clothing manufacturers really succeed in
selling their products abroad are the Dominions, where there is
a fair demand from newly-arrived Englishmen ; especially has
this been the case with South Africa and Australia, neither of
which until recently have been highly industrialized; but even
these countries are rapidly becoming self-supporting. Returning to Messrs. Barrans, we may add that the conditions under
which the work is done leave very little to be desired. The
factory was specially built for the purpose to which it is being
put, and the workrooms are large, well-lighted and well-
ventilated. Cloak-room accommodation is adequate, and rest-
rooms and a dining-room are provided, where meals can be
purchased at very moderate rates or the employees' own food
can be warmed up gratis. Similar conditions are to be found in
many large establishments ; on the other hand, there are
factories in Leeds, and still more in other towns, of which
nothing of the sort can be said.

In the same line of business as Barrans are several smaller
firms, whose hands number anything from 200 to 500 or more.
Some of these boast an antiquity nearly as great, others have
only been in existence for twenty or thirty years ; in nearly
every case they are in the hands of the second generation of

owners. Typical of these is Messrs. David Little & Co., an old-established family business, employing 200 work-people, and turning out a slightly lower grade of article than Barrans, exclusively for the home market. Like all but the mammoth establishments, Little's is a private firm.

A comparatively recent development has been the growth of manufacturing businesses which maintain their own retail shops. Firms of the Barran and Little type dispose of their goods mostly to customers with whom they have a very old connection, through the medium of showrooms or travellers, or both. Messrs. Barran, for instance, have a very attractive showroom on the premises, where single garments may be purchased by regular customers or orders for large consignments received. Messrs. Little have branches for selling purposes in Edinburgh, Cardiff, Liverpool, Nottingham and Newcastle. On the other hand, the newer firms with their own retail shops usually dispose of their entire output direct to the consumer through this channel. The most remarkable establishment of this type has had a career which can only be described as startling. It was founded by a Jewish manufacturer, originally in a very small way of business, who came to the fore during the Great War. In a few years he has built up from tiny beginnings an undertaking which provides employment for nearly 4000 people on the manufacturing side alone, besides those employed in the retail shops, whose numbers must run into several hundreds. His name, or rather the name under which his firm is registered, is familiar to almost every man, woman and child in the country, and stands out in glittering letters on the shop-fronts of his establishments in the principal thoroughfares of all our cities and towns. The trade he carries on is exclusively of the " wholesale bespoke " variety. A customer can enter one of the retail shops, say in Plymouth or Aberdeen, choose the material for a suit or coat, have his measurements taken, and on the following day the order will have reached the factory on the outskirts of Leeds. Here, in the two vast single-story sheds which comprise the greater part of the premises, well lit by virtue of their glass roofs, the order will be executed without delay. In one room the cutting is done with the aid of an enormous stock of patterns. The pattern nearest to the customer's measurements is selected and such adjustments as are necessary are made by the individual cutter. On the following day, perhaps, the material, with the requisite linings, etc., will be in the hands of the machinists, and after passing through twenty or thirty different processes will emerge as a complete suit, made-to-measure, or more or less to measure, for fifty shillings, and ready for dispatch to the branch where it was ordered. At the branch the innocent customer can try it on, any minor alterations required can readily be done on the premises, and within a week the suit will be paid for and in the customer's possession. This type of firm depends for its success on the vast working-class and lower middle-class market for which it caters, and on the policy of never allowing credit. The wholesale clothiers, who do not sell direct to the public, but to retail outfitters, are compelled to allow their customers credit, since these latter are by old-established tradition themselves obliged to wait, sometimes for a considerable period, before receiving payment for the clothes they sell. While the multiple-shop firms, on the other hand, have succeeded in building up a purely cash trade, it may be suspected that, in view of their enormous turnover, they are in a position at times to exact credit from the cloth manufacturer. In this way they are enabled to do a very large trade indeed on the basis of somewhat slender capital resources. Those who are aware that the demand for clothes is highly seasonal may well ask how such an establishment succeeds in keeping its workers fully employed if its entire trade is " wholesale bespoke," and accordingly no garments are made for stock. The answer is a twofold one. In the first place, the demand for clothes on the part of the working-man is far less seasonal than is that of the patron of Savile Row or Hanover Square. Secondly, in the case at least of the particular firm in question, the problem of seasonal fluctuations has very largely been met by frequent dismissals and re-engagements of its employees—a practice less conducive to their financial prosperity than to its own. During the past few years the labour market in Leeds, as elsewhere, has been overcrowded, and thus in a particularly suitable condition for this practice, which may not prove so feasible when hands grow scarcer. Firms with a reputation for keeping their hands on all the year round may then reap the reward of their public spirit. Besides maintaining a fluctuating number of work-people, this firm also indulges in the practice which is still common, though not so universal as it used to be, of giving out work, in rush periods, especially trouser-finishing, to outworkers or small Jewish middlemen. Similar, but less spectacular, has been the success of several other multiple-shop clothiers in Leeds. Some of them have attempted to combine the practice of selling through their own shops with that of obtaining custom from tailors, but seldom with success, as their would-be customers not unnaturally regard them as unwarranted intruders on other people's preserves. Many of them, also, make a good many garments for stock, especially overcoats, instead of confining their attention to the made-to-measure trade.

Though men's tailoring is the mainstay of the Leeds clothing industry, at least one of the larger manufacturers is engaged in the mantle trade. This firm turns out a first-rate garment, finding its customers largely in the department stores of big towns, with whom it deals both through a staff of travellers and through showrooms in Leeds and London. The bulk of the trade is ready-made, but there is a small bespoke department. There is also a not very important overseas trade.

The conditions of employment reach well up to the highest standard set by the large men's clothiers.

A day or two in Leeds would suffice to visit the fifteen or twenty well-known clothing factories within whose walls the greater proportion of the trade is concentrated. A whole year might fail to reveal some of the little businesses hidden away in quarters of the town not likely to be frequented by the casual stranger, or stuck almost under his very nose behind some block of warehouses in the centre of the city. Most of these smaller factories follow the big firms in confining themselves to men's clothing, but there is also a sprinkling of small blouse and skirt manufacturers. One skirt firm, for instance, is situated in extremely dingy and cramped quarters on the upper floors of a warehouse in the centre of the town. From every point of view it affords a striking contrast with the giant firms we described in the men's tailoring trade. While some, at least, of the latter have an elaborate system of cost-accounting, the manager of this skirt firm told me that he had practically no idea of the cost to him of any individual garment, or even of a complete order. All he reckoned to do was to make a certain net profit at the end of the year, fixing his prices more or less by rule of thumb, after the manner of the average farmer. Though his relations with his employees seemed to be on a very friendly footing, he had apparently never even heard of the existence of the Trade Boards and, from the figures he quoted, was certainly not paying Trade Board wages. He had a genial and sympathetic personality, which evidently made up in the eyes of his work-people for their low wages, long hours, and gloomy surroundings. Altogether he employed well over a hundred hands, all but two or three of them women, none of whom, it need scarcely be added, were members of a union. His office staff consisted of himself, a sort of all-round handy-man, and a couple of shorthand typists. I mention him here, not as an example of a " bad employer," which he most assuredly was not, but of an " ignorant employer," which he equally certainly was, and of whom there must be a goodly number lurking in the backwaters of the trade, though it is difficult for a temporary visitor to locate them.

A still smaller type of establishment to be found in Leeds is the workshop of the Jewish subcontractor. In most of the larger towns Jewish small masters are to be found, but in most cases they work for the retail trade, as for instance in London, where, as we shall see, they are particularly numerous, and where their undertakings often reach quite considerable proportions. In other cases Jewish masters deal directly with the wholesale merchant houses ; this is common in Manchester in the raincoat trade, and is also found in London. In Leeds, on the other hand, the Jewish tailors, with a staff not usually exceeding a dozen or fifteen, execute orders, especially in the wholesale bespoke trade, for the larger manufacturers, who, of course, supply the materials, and on whose premises the work is sometimes, though not usually, executed. These sub-contractors always employ Jewish labour. With regard to the labour employed by the larger firms, it is interesting to note that in Leeds most employers make no distinction between Jew and Gentile. Only a few refuse to allow the two races to work side by side, though this refusal is the almost universal custom in London. Those who still maintain the distinction claim that it is essential for the maintenance of harmonious relations in the factory ; they also assert that the Jewish men are untidy and dirty in their habits.

There has been a tendency in recent years for the men's clothing trade to become more and more concentrated in Leeds at the expense of other centres, especially of Bristol. This is an easily understood development. The high degree of concentration already to be found in Leeds creates many advantages for the manufacturer, which he will not find elsewhere. Chief among these is the highly-specialized labour market. In most centres the employer in need of fresh hands has to engage any clothing operative who may present himself, irrespective of the type of job to which he or she has been previously accustomed. In Leeds, on the other hand, a manufacturer will advertise for a man or woman with experience in a firm doing just his own class of trade, who has been employed on exactly the processes for which he requires additional labour. The evening editions of the local papers all contain long columns of advertisements for clothing operatives of various kinds, a glance down which will reveal how minute this specialization has become. Whether it is fraught with gain or loss for the worker, thus condemned to spend her industrial life at a job which never varies from month to month or from year to year, is a moot point, but it is certainly an advantage from the employer's point of view. Akin to the advantage afforded by the specialized labour market is that provided by the highly-developed cloth-marketing arrangements, which enable the clothing manufacturer to select his materials with a minimum of delay and inconvenience. He is also in close contact with any new developments in technique that may arise, and, generally speaking, shares in the innumerable and often intangible advantages which come from the existence of a local tradition and a local atmosphere around his trade.

The conditions just described also favour a high degree of organization, among the employers as among the employed. Among the former, there are two powerful bodies, the Whole-sale Clothiers' Association and the Northern Clothiers' Association. The organized workers belong to the Tailors' and Garment Workers' Trade Union, of which Leeds is the headquarters. There is a separate section for the Jewish workers, who at one time had an independent union of their own, which was merged in the larger body during the war. This Jewish section has its own club-house in the part of the city once known as the Ghetto, in which the bulk of the Jewish population still lives. Most of the Jewish operatives, women as well as men, have been drawn into the union. Among the Gentiles this is not the case, the women being rather poorly organized, and in sections other than the men's tailoring trade hardly so at all. In consequence of the strength of the union locally wages are good, often being fixed by agreement somewhat above Trade Board rates. Conditions in factories are normally good, too, but housing conditions, especially in the Jewish quarter, are a disgrace. Leeds has the unsavoury reputation of having a larger proportion of back-to-back houses than any other town in the British Isles, with the exception of Glasgow. Even so, it is said that there has been an improvement since the beginning of the century. The general impression the visitor to the town carries away with him is one of sordid prosperity and efficiency, of a well-fed and well-dressed population, living in a town of mean houses, squalid streets and gaunt, smoke-belching factories—a hideous picture of mid-Victorian industrialism at its worst.

THE HUDDERSFIELD AND HALIFAX DISTRICT

Turning our backs on Leeds and its equally ugly sister, Bradford, we come to the comparatively attractive clothing towns which lie on the western confines of the West Riding. After a week or two, in which one's lungs seem to have become permanently choked in the fumes of chemical works and tanneries, it is a relief to breathe the strong moorland air of Halifax or Huddersfield or Hebden Bridge. To one unaccustomed to the North, a note of harshness is struck by all these grey northern towns, with their stone houses and cobbled streets and the bleak surrounding moors. But at least those we are now dealing with are clean, clean as only a town on a weather-beaten sea-coast or in a wind-swept and rain-beaten upland country can be. Here, on the steep hill-sides or at their feet beside running brooks are the factories where corduroys and moleskins are made, as well as a variety of other low-grade and medium-grade garments.

Huddersfield is the least characteristic town of this district. On a small scale, it does a trade similar to that carried on at Leeds, a medium as well as a high-class men's tailoring trade, employing about 2500 workers, which calls for no special comment. The neighbouring town of Halifax is more interesting. There are not very many firms here, nor are they very large, but almost each establishment has its own special class of trade. Altogether about 2000 workers are employed. Men's tailoring is practically non-existent. Nearly all the firms are engaged in the manufacture of women's clothes of cotton, silk, flannelette and other light materials. White (calico) goods are made on a fairly large scale, though most of the firms which used to confine themselves to this trade are turning their attention now to blouses, jumpers, cotton and silk dresses, etc, for which there is a steady and increasing demand both in summer and winter. These articles are mostly made in the work-rooms of large stores in London, Manchester, Glasgow and elsewhere, but smaller shops buy from factories such as those at Halifax and Manchester.

A few miles from Halifax, and connected with it by a tram-line, is the valley in which are situated the villages of Sowerby Bridge, Mytholmroyd and Hebden Bridge, in which, particularly in the latter, is centred the once prosperous but now declining manufacture of cords and moles. The decline of this trade is due to the change which has come in the habits of working-men in regard to dress during the past quarter of a century. There is still, however, a small demand for these clothes ; apart from meeting this demand the Hebden Bridge now make bluettes, engineers' and other overalls, boys' knickers, " Kafir goods," and so on. The trade is a poor-class one, but the efficiency of the factories is of a high order. Of these there are about a dozen all told, providing work for the whole industrial population of the place. One or two are branches of Leeds wholesale clothing firms, one belongs to the Co-operative Wholesale Society, the others have been built up from small beginnings by working men. Shut in by the hills which tower on every side, this valley is singularly undisturbed by the industrial troubles of the outside world. Few of the masters are wealthy men, most of them belong to very nearly the same social class as their employees, and relations between them are consequently exceptionally cordial. It is interesting to note that Hebden Bridge shares with Wigan the distinction of being one of the only two towns in England in which the clothing workers are organized in trade unions on a 100 per cent. or anything like 100 per cent. basis. A fuller account of this interesting district will be found in R. H. Tawney's *Minimum Rates in the Tailoring Trade.*

MANCHESTER AND DISTRICT

Next to Leeds, Manchester is the most important clothing centre in the North of England. Indeed the absolute number of workers employed is somewhat larger, though they form a smaller percentage of the total population—nearly 40,000 out of 800,000. To these we may add 5000 in Salford and 4000 —mainly in the hat and cap trade—in Stockport, both these towns being coterminous with Manchester. Numerically most important, in Manchester as in Leeds, are the trades classed under "Tailoring" in the Census classification—namely, retail and wholesale tailoring, and mantle-making. There are several factories of the Leeds type, most of which date back some thirty years. None are so old-established as the older Leeds firms, which had been in existence at least thirty years before the wholesale tailoring trade spread to Manchester.

On the other hand, there are not so many recently-founded firms. The average Manchester establishment employs about 300 hands, and none of them approach in size the Leeds giants. A very thriving branch in recent years has been the raincoat trade, mostly in the hands of Jewish employers. Sometimes raincoats are made, as they are in Leeds, as a side-line by the wholesale clothiers ; but more usually the trade is an entirely specialized one. It is carried on largely under poor conditions, in the upper floors of tumble-down houses in the Ancoats district. To a considerable extent, the raincoat manufacturers are men who made money during the war on Government work, often as subcontractors, and who turned their attention to raincoats when war-time orders ceased. In this branch of the industry, the export market in America and South Africa is a large one, and is said to offer further opportunities for development. The total numbers of workers engaged in this trade is about 5000.

In the wholesale mantle trade, Manchester rivals Leeds both in the number of work-people engaged and the quality of the garments turned out. The numbers employed amount to about 2000. One of the most important mantle factories is that of the Co-operative Wholesale Society, which is situated at Broughton and employs 300 hands. In this establishment, the problem of seasonal fluctuations, always particularly difficult in the women's trades, is largely met by confining bulk orders, including large numbers of women's raincoats, to the slack periods, and executing only " special " (i.e. wholesale bespoke) orders during the rush months.

In all sections of the " tailoring " trades, Jewish sub-contractors are to be found in large, but slowly decreasing, numbers. The considerable Jewish population in Manchester is, in fact, principally engaged in some kind of tailoring. The typical establishment consists of six or a dozen girls working under the Jewish master in a small tenement workshop, frequently under very bad conditions.

D

In addition to the above, there is a fairly strong contingent of handicraft tailors—say 300 to 400 in all. Manchester, indeed, is the site of the headquarters of the Trade Union catering for this section of the clothing trades—The Amalgamated Society of Tailors and Tailoresses. At the time of the formation of the union shortly after the middle of the nineteenth century, the handicraft tailor still maintained his position unimpaired throughout the land. It was thus not especially remarkable that the capital city of a densely populated industrial district, surrounded by a galaxy of towns and villages, should witness the formation of a union which aimed at and ultimately succeeded in embracing the whole country in its scope ; though even then London might appear to have been the most favourable location for such a body. At the present time, when handicraft tailoring outside the West End is dead or dying, it is quite anomalous that the head office of the union should be situated in a provincial centre. As in the case of the United Garment Workers' headquarters at Leeds, the circumstance must be regarded to-day as a historical accident.

The underclothing trade used to be a very important one, but is now going down. Before the war there were large export markets in Europe, Australia, and South Africa. All of these have fallen off, owing to reduced purchasing power in Europe and to the very heavy tariffs on made-up goods which have recently been imposed in the colonies. Fashions in underclothes have also changed. The quantity worn has been considerably reduced, and woven garments of artificial silk have had an immense vogue, which at present shows few signs of dying. None the less, Manchester still boasts many firms which manufacture underclothing, commonly turning out outer garments of light materials as well. For these trades it remains the most important single centre in the country. The trade is seasonal, crêpe-de-chine, silk, calico, etc., being popular for summer wear, while winceyettes, flannelettes and flannel are required in autumn and winter. Frequently handkerchiefs and pillow-cases are made by the same firms, though the methods employed in the manufacture of these articles are sufficiently specialized to call for a separate staff. This is unfortunate, as it precludes the possibility of using them as a means of providing employment for the workers in the other sections in slack times. The plain hemming of sheets, on the other hand, is an easily acquired art, and is therefore commonly performed in slack periods by the girls who are usually engaged in making underclothes. It may be added, that in the past, the underclothing trade gave employment to large numbers of home-workers under very sweated conditions. A woman would be given a sample garment to copy and supplied with all materials, including any embroidery necessary. Thus the work was easy and the demand for it correspondingly great. Nowadays the factories are half empty and there is consequently no employment for the home-worker.

The next most important section in Manchester is the shirt and collar trade, employing perhaps 6000 workers. Here also recent years have seen a waning prosperity. During the war there was an almost insatiable demand for army shirts from the War Office. Much homework sprang into being, under bad conditions, at which the Government Inspectors were inclined to wink. Before the war homework had been dying out, and since 1918 it has again diminished though not entirely disappeared. As in the case of the underclothing trade, the colonial market has been severely hit by recently imposed tariffs on made-up as opposed to piece-goods. This has specially affected the low-class trade, of which Manchester was at one time the centre. It is this trade that is in the hands of subcontractors, who in turn give out work to married women, paying them 1s. to 1s. 6d. a dozen out of the 3s. which they themselves receive. Perhaps the best foreign market remaining is to be found in the Scandinavian countries, though even here competition, especially from German sources, is severe. A second blow to the Manchester trade has been dealt by changing fashions. In the old days there was a large demand for flannel shirts, except in the summer months, but in the last fifteen years the tunic-shirt, of cotton material, has risen rapidly to popularity for all-the-year-round wear. It might be expected that, since Manchester is the metropolis of the cotton industries, conditions would be particularly favourable for the manufacture of cotton shirts. In point of fact, though these are now made by several local firms, there is severe competition from other centres, including Glasgow, Nottingham and London—not to mention Derry in Northern Ireland, where tunic-shirts were first introduced. Dress shirts and linen collars are less in demand than they once were ; those that are now made are very seldom of linen, but of cotton material "fired" to look like linen. Men's pyjamas are usually also made by the shirt and collar firms. Women's pyjamas, which have to be trimmed with lace or embroidery, on the other hand, are made by underclothing manufacturers. Conditions inside the shirt factories have undergone continuous improvement since 1905. Wages, under agreements with the local branch of the Tailors' and Garment Workers' Union, are generally slightly in excess of the Trade Board rates.

The last section which calls for notice among the Manchester clothing trades is light dressmaking, including the manufacture of blouses. Much of this is in the hands of firms of the type of Tootal, Broadhurst, Lee & Co., which not only makes up the garments ready for sale, but itself manufactures the materials from which they are made, and does a huge home and export trade both in piece-goods and finished garments of all kinds. Messrs. Rylands Limited do a similar trade, though it forms only a part of their activities as general warehousemen. In addition, several of the big retail stores have large workshops attached to their premises after the London fashion. High-grade goods are made by smaller firms, with perhaps fifty hands in the workrooms on the upper floors, a showroom on the first floor and a shop beneath. Part of the output is sold in the shop, and part is bought for high-class retail establishments in other towns by travellers who visit the showroom. As often as not, millinery is combined with dressmaking, though the two sections are of course separately staffed. The finer grades of underwear are also commonly made by firms of this type. The wages earned by the staff are very high, and there is a brisk competition to enter the trade, in spite of the long period of learnership on low pay which this involves. In fact it is generally impossible for a girl much over fourteen to find an opening, as it is not worth the employers' while to pay the rates which the Trade Board imposes for learners above this age.

Other clothing trades in the district are hats and caps, especially at Stockport and Denton, and corsets. The former provide work for about 6000 and the latter for about 1000 people. Neither of these, however, come strictly within the purview of our enquiry.

With Manchester we have included the other Lancashire towns. Of these the most important are Liverpool with about 10,000 workers in tailoring and dressmaking, Blackburn with 6000, Wigan with 3000, and Preston. Liverpool is especially notable for the excellence of its retail tailoring, in respect of which it ranks after the West End, but probably in front of Manchester, and certainly of any other provincial centre in England. The trade finds its customers among the wealthy business families of the town. The number of Jewish sub-contractors is also considerable. There are five or six clothing factories employing an average of 400 hands apiece. The largest and most up-to-date of these is the one recently erected by Messrs. Lewis Limited, the well-known department store,

with branches in Manchester, Birmingham, and Liverpool. In
this establishment the very latest machinery is in use, and
American methods of high-speed mass production prevail.
Other firms are the Donegal Tweed Company, which does
not confine itself to the materials implied by its name, and
John Peck & Co., which specializes in dungarees.

Blackburn and Preston call for no comments, but Wigan
is an interesting centre. We have already noted the fact that
the comparatively small number of workers—slightly over
2000—in this town have been organized on what is practically
a 100 per cent. basis by the Tailors' and Garment Workers'
Trade Union. The credit for this is chiefly due to the energy
of one man, Councillor Smith, who dominates the local Labour
and Trade Union movement. With the exception of a few
journeymen tailors, the unorganized workers are exclusively
women, and number about fifty in the wholesale tailoring
trade, together with perhaps 200 in the light clothing trade.
The former trade is in the hands of two firms, Messrs. Coop
and Messrs. Brown and Haig, the former with 1200 and the
latter with 400 workers, both of which make exclusively
bespoke garments, the ready-made trade having disappeared
from the town. At one time Coops executed contract work
and shipping orders, though now it does so no longer. There
is a goodclass mantle trade, employing about 500 workers,
fully organized, while another 300 are engaged in the manufacture of various types of light clothing — baby-linen,
underclothing, shirts, blouses and overalls. Unlike the big
cities, such as Leeds, Manchester, Birmingham, or Liverpool,
Wigan has almost no Jewish workers—perhaps half a dozen
subcontractors employing a few girls on their own premises.
At one time subcontracting, especially in the mantle and
dressmaking trades, was quite common, but has now nearly
died out. In all sections wages are good, averaging 25 per
cent. to 30 per cent. above Trade Board rates, and conditions

of work excellent. Homework is almost non-existent. In fact,
if in all clothing towns the lot of the worker was as good as
it is in Wigan, there would seem to be little need for the
existence of Trade Boards in the industry, or for the use of
the term " sweating " in connection with it.

THE WEST MIDLANDS

The West Midlands as a clothing district may be divided into
two parts : Crewe and The Potteries on the one hand, and
Birmingham and the surrounding district on the other.

In the former the most important centres are Crewe and
Newcastle-under-Lyme.   In both these towns the trade is
largely of the contract type. Crewe has a factory owned by the
London, Midland and Scottish Railway Co., making uniforms
for its employees. There is also in the district a shirt trade
of some importance, located at Crewe and Nantwich, a small
town near-by. In all these cases the organization of the workers
is weak, and wages are consequently none too high.   Trade
Board rates are, however, commonly paid and complaints of
evasion are few. The reason for the weakness of trade unionism
is probably twofold. First comes the fact that the type of
trade carried on calls only for a low degree of skill, whereas it
is principally in the higher grades that organization makes
permanent headway.   More important is the fact that the
district is one where trade unionism is poorly developed in all
sections of industry. It consists of a mass of small straggling
towns without any clearly marked centre, such as is provided
by Manchester for the cotton district or by Birmingham
farther south. There is no single staple industry employing
highly-skilled operatives with a powerful union round whose
banner workers in other trades might rally. In a great many
of the miscellaneous trades characteristic of this squalid
district, which has been immortalized by Arnold Bennett in

his " Five Towns " series of novels, the dominant figure is the small master risen from the ranks ; and where he flourishes the soil for trade unionism is seldom propitious. As compared with other centres, the clothing trade has here suffered rather severely from the post-war slump, and unemployment is exceptionally serious. Contract work naturally declines or flourishes according as industrial conditions are gloomy or the reverse, to a far more marked degree than work for the private purchaser. Simultaneously with the reduced home demand there has been a further reduction in output, due to the loss of export markets which used to absorb a not inconsiderable proportion of the clothing produced in the district.

The Birmingham area is more interesting. Birmingham itself is the principal centre with about 11,000 employees. Next in order come Walsall with 2500, Dudley with 1500, Wolverhampton and Nuneaton. The most compact of these is Walsall, where there are two or three fairly large firms doing a medium men's and boys' wholesale trade. Both here and at Dudley there was at one time a brisk export trade, especially to Canada, which has now died out, and the industry is in a stationary condition which calls for little comment. Wolverhampton is only of minor importance, having one clothing factory, while Nuneaton has a few small firms making men's clothing and shirts.

Turning to the 11,000 clothing workers in Birmingham itself, the first thing one should notice is that this figure is a very small fraction of the million odd to which the total population amounts. The clothing industry is merely one of the almost innumerable others carried on in the city, instead of occupying, as in Leeds, East London, and even Manchester, a prominent place in the pageant of municipal life. The next thing that strikes one is the relatively important part played by the subdivisional trade working for retailers in the neighbourhood. Altogether some 6000 persons are thus employed, mostly making men's clothes, though a few are working for the mantle trade. This compares with a total of handicraft tailors unexpectedly small for a city of the size of Birmingham, and of its importance as a shopping centre for the thickly populated surrounding area. The reason is probably to be sought in the fact that London is within easy reach, so that the sort of man who buys expensive clothes often prefers to go to the West End for them. The poorer man with fewer opportunities for visits to town buys them locally, so providing work for the subcontractors. These last are mostly Jews, but include a small proportion of Gentiles. They usually live and work on the same premises, and are principally to be found in a district in the centre of the town, consisting of two or three streets, in which nearly every house is occupied by one or more of them. This district is not an unpleasant one, and it may be said that conditions in the workshops are above the average found in other comparable towns, such as Liverpool, Hull, or Manchester. Before dealing with the wholesale trade, we might add that some of the large retail drapers and department stores naturally maintain their own dressmaking and millinery workshops. In the main, however, they confine themselves to having alterations done on the premises and purchase their stock from wholesale houses.

In the Wholesale trade, Men's and Boys' Clothing occupies the chief place in Birmingham as in the neighbouring towns. mantles are of some importance, while baby - linen, light dressmaking and millinery establishments are also to be found. The men's firms are of medium size and do a medium class of trade. The average number of employees is a few hundred on the premises, together with a fair proportion of outworkers. In the mantle trade there is only one factory of any importance, with about 400 hands. The other trades above mentioned employ perhaps 2000 hands in the wholesale section between them,

Except in the case of one firm, which is practically a closed shop, the workers are badly organized in the wholesale clothing trade, and practically not at all in the other sections. This is partly due to the fact that the chief union—the Tailors' and Garment Workers' Trade Union—has to contend with the rivalry of various general unions, a rivalry which it does not have to face where the clothing trades occupy a more prominent position. It is also due to the weakness in the neighbourhood of trade unionism in general, which is as marked in Birmingham as in the Potteries, and for the same reasons. Outside the T. & G.W.T.U. and the general unions there is a membership of the A.S.T. & T. which can be counted on the fingers of one's two hands. At one time the Jewish subdivisional workers had an organization of their own, the " Jewish International Tailors' and Pressers' Union," which has now almost disappeared. In spite of this weakness of organization, working conditions are well up to the standard of other large towns and wages, which before the passing of the Trade Boards Acts were very low, have much improved. At the same time evasion of Trade Board rates does sometimes occur by the use of the device of checking out. Under this system a worker will come to the factory in the morning and be given, say, an hour's work. Then she has to clock out for perhaps a couple of hours, until more work is available, and thus is not paid for that period, although actually she has to remain on the premises all the time. In places where the unions' influence is considerable the practice is kept down ; elsewhere, as in Birmingham, it remains rampant.

Out of the total number of workers employed, some 1000 are outworkers—usually whole families living and working together. Very few of these are Jews. Their numbers have been reduced in recent years and their earnings have been much improved from the very low level at which they stood at the time of the publication in 1907 of Messrs. Cadbury, Matheson and Shann's study of industrial conditions in Birmingham, under the title *Women's Work and Wages*. Some of the home-workers live right outside the town—often between five and ten miles—and come in periodically by tram to fetch the work. They are particularly numerous in the outlying town of Bromsgrove, a small place about eight miles to the south-west, where also there is a solitary clothing factory, a branch of a Birmingham firm.

Generally speaking, we may regard the Birmingham district as one in which the clothing trades are of small and declining importance. Most of the existing firms date back some thirty years, and, while new ones are seldom founded, every now and then an old establishment is closed down. The Co-operative Wholesale Society, for instance, maintained a large blouse, apron and pinafore factory until 1926, when it was shut down, and a similar fate has overtaken other concerns doing the same class of trade. The healthiest section is men's clothing, though even here the volume of trade is not what it used to be. The output in all lines is quite insufficient to meet the needs of the district, which are largely filled from Leeds and elsewhere. It is therefore only natural to find that there is little export to other centres, either at home or abroad. Some firms sell as far afield as South Wales, but more commonly they find a market nearer home. The South African and South American trades, which at one time were of some importance, have died out completely.

BRISTOL AND THE SOUTH-WEST

As befits the largest town of a district where once was situated the chief woollen industry of the country, Bristol is a clothing centre of considerable importance. Before the Industrial Revolution the West of England was a very im-portant centre of population, with Bristol the second or third largest city in the country and, after London, the leading port. In those days the clothiers of Gloucestershire were famous the world over. Since then, the glory has departed. None the less, there were sufficient remnants of the cloth industry in existence in the third quarter of the nineteenth century to make Bristol one of the first districts in which large clothing factories were built.

The total number employed in the clothing trades in Bristol itself is about 9000. Of these 2000 are in the retail trade, handicraft or subdivisional, 4000 in the men's and boys' wholesale trade, 1000 in the corset trade, and the balance in dressmaking, millinery, etc. Other clothing towns in the south-west are Taunton, with large shirt and collar factories ; Bridgewater, with a shirt, collar and underlinen trade ; Bath, with a men's clothing trade and a few shirt factories ; Stroud, with men's clothing ; Gloucester, only of slight importance ; Swindon, with a railway factory; and, finally, Plymouth, where there are as many as 2000 workers in the men's trade.

In the men's trade Bristol ranks next in importance after Leeds, London, and Manchester. The market chiefly catered for is the superior working-class one, while there are also a number of contract-houses, mainly making police-uniforms. Since the war four or five firms have closed down. This may partly be due to the universal trade slump, partly to the increasing competition, in the south-west of England as else-where, of multiple firms supplied from factories in Leeds, and partly to the loss of the export trade which, owing to Bristol's position as a seaport, was formerly of considerable magnitude, but amounts now to not a tenth of what it was twenty years ago. The only factory which has been established of recent years is that of the Co-operative Wholesale Society, the advent of which has been a boon to many workers displaced by firms which have lately closed down.

In spite of, or perhaps because of, this falling off in the trade, conditions are quite fair, the amount of outwork having diminished, though by no means entirely ceased. Trouser-making, in particular, is still often done out, especially in the neighbouring villages, such as Winterbourne. Exact information on the subject is, however, difficult to get. Trade Union organization is fairly good, the United Garment Workers, as in Leeds, London, and Manchester, maintaining a full-time Secretary at Bristol. Altogether the local branch of the union contains well over 2000 members. Wages are standardized at Trade Board rates, and only in rare cases—usually of cutters' rates—are they any higher. In the waterproof section, which is not under the jurisdiction of the Trade Board, they are apt to be low. A notable feature of the retail trade, compared with that of other large towns, is the scarcity of Jewish sub-contractors. This was not always so, for at one time there were a great many Jews, many of whose workshops were notoriously cramped and insanitary. Those who are now left are said to maintain a decent standard, both in regard to the condition of their premises and the wages they pay to their employees. The handicraft section of the retail trade is small, consisting only of a few shops in the fashionable suburb of Clifton, where custom is provided by the large population of retired professional men, as also by the well-known public school. A few of the employees of these firms are members of the A.S.T. & T.

In Stroud there are three clothing firms employing, between them, about 1500 people. At one time the bulk of the trade was in the hands of Jewish subcontractors, who had the work done by home-workers in the surrounding villages, fetching it themselves from the factories and distributing it to the work-people. This practice has now entirely disappeared. Conditions of work and rates of pay, which used to be notoriously bad, are now up to the general standard prevailing in other centres.

Generally speaking, what is true in regard to conditions in Bristol and Stroud is true of the whole of the south-west ; there has been a vast improvement in recent years. The town to which this verdict is least applicable is undoubtedly Plymouth. Why this should be so it is hard to see. Perhaps the explanation is to be found in the fact that here, as in Portsmouth, an atmosphere of naval discipline prevails and has fostered a domineering spirit among the local employers and one of subordination among their work-people. A further point in the same connection is that the place is an isolated industrial centre, far from the homelands of Trade Unionism in the Midlands and the North, and though attempts have from time to time been made to organize the garment workers, the measure of success met with has been small. The trade is confined to men's and boys' wholesale tailoring, much of the work being on War Office contracts, though some firms work for the civilian market and claim to turn out a first-rate article.

SOUTH WALES

Like all the important centres of population in the country, South Wales boasts its clothing trades, though they play a relatively insignificant part in the industrial life of the district. They are carried on in the three principal towns—Cardiff, Swansea and Newport.

Cardiff has 1700 workers in the tailoring and rather fewer in the light dressmaking trades. Unlike Bristol, this and the other South Wales towns have large numbers of Jewish sub-contractors, who carry on a high-class subdivisional trade. The wages paid are high, but the conditions of work frequently poor. Swansea in particular is notorious for the wretched premises in which much of the work is done—high up in old tenement houses which a fire would convert into a death-trap. Some of the factory trade is of a very low class, and includes the making of overalls and dungarees. As a light dress-making centre Cardiff ranks next in point of numbers after Manchester and about on a level with Nottingham. The trade is a relatively low-class one, the materials mostly employed being cottons and flannelettes. The shirt trade is represented by a single factory, that of the Co-operative Wholesale Society. In nearly all cases the work is turned out exclusively for the local market, there being no exports now to speak of. Like the Birmingham area, South Wales is not self-supporting in the matter of clothes, and goes for what is not made locally to Leeds, Manchester, and London. This is only natural, since in neither district are textiles manufactured. Indeed we may almost say, that with the single exception of London, there is no really important clothing centre situated very far from the seat of manufacture of one or other of the raw materials, wool or cotton or linen, principally employed. For this reason the north-east coast has even less claim to rank as a clothing centre than has South Wales.

THE EAST MIDLANDS

There are several towns in this district where clothing of one sort or another is manufactured, though many of them may be dismissed in a few words. Nottingham, Leicester, Kettering, Wellingborough, and Northampton are the most noteworthy.

Northampton is a town of mixed industries, the principal of which, as every schoolboy knows, is boots. Apart from the inevitable retail tailors, here as everywhere else a declining body of skilled handicraftsmen, the clothing industry is represented by about 1200 workers in the light dressmaking and blouse trades.

Kettering and Wellingborough, the former mainly a boot town, and the latter largely devoting itself to engineering, iron-smelting and flour-milling, make men's and boys' clothing, the numbers employed in the two places being respectively 5000 and about 4000. An interesting point about Kettering is that, together with Plymouth and Huddersfield, it is one of the towns where the handicraft union, the A.S.T. & T., has organized or attempted to organize the factory workers, a task usually left to the T. & G.W.T.U. At the moment it has achieved but a modest success, with only about 20 per cent. of the employees organized. It is, however, fair to add that this figure is as good as that attained by the Garment Workers in all but the best organized towns.

It may seem strange that clothing factories should be established in towns of the above type, where at first sight there would seem to be neither historical nor economic reasons for them. They are not important centres of population, nor are they situated in the neighbourhood of an existing or former textile manufacturing district. The reason must probably be sought in the favourable labour market of the locality. Both these towns have staple trades, where a large proportion of men is required, more especially Wellingborough, with its ironworks. It is thus possible to tap a fairly plentiful supply of female labour. Furthermore, the countryside in the neighbourhood is well populated and the wives and daughters of the badly-paid agricultural labourers can often be engaged at far lower rates of wages than would have to be offered in a place like Leeds, where competition for hands is keener. This last factor is responsible for the existence of many isolated clothing factories in rural or semi-rural districts in the south and east of England.

A further point of some interest arises with regard to the labour-force in Kettering, a point which has its counterpart in other places with regard to other trades. The girls in the factories commonly oscillate between the clothing and boot trades, especially during the learnership stage of their careers, in the hope that when one is depressed they may be able to find employment as qualified hands in the other. The same general idea is involved in the practice of manufacturers engaged in the production of goods for which the demand is only a seasonal one, of finding some alternative article which they can turn out in the off-season. A well-known example is the straw-hat trade at Luton, which has taken to making felt and cloth head-gear for the winter season as well as straw for the summer. The processes involved in the two trades are of course quite different, the only connection between them being that they cater for alternating and mutually exclusive needs. The practice developed by the Kettering workers has much less to be said for it. If there were any causal connection between periods of activity in the clothing trade and of depression in the boot trade, or *vice versa*, it would be an admirable institution, but there seems to be no very adequate reason for supposing that such connection exists. On the contrary, the briskness of demand both for boots and clothing depends mainly on the available purchasing power in the pockets of the wage-earning classes, and this in turn on the general volume of trade activity. They are thus likely to be depressed or active simultaneously rather than alternately. It may be added that the same phenomenon is observable to a lesser degree at Northampton, where the protagonists are the boot operatives and the blouse and dressmaking operatives.

Leicester, while it takes first place as a hosiery centre, is of no very great importance in connection with the sewing trades. There are, however, about 3000 workers in tailoring, wholesale and retail, mostly the former. The largest firm in the town—Messrs. Hart & Levy—enjoys a very wide reputation for the quality of its products. The Census returns show just over 1000 hands employed in " Dress, Blouse and Millinery." For the most part these are not engaged in the making of garments cut from cotton or other textile material,

E

but in producing underclothes from knitted fabrics, to an increasing degree now from artificial silk, a process which, as is elsewhere pointed out, is quite distinct, and constitutes a separate trade.

Nottingham, on the other hand, though clothing is not the chief industry of the town, is a centre of growing importance in the light dressmaking trades. There are a few small wholesale tailoring factories employing altogether about 2000 hands, though in this respect Leicester is more important. The retail section includes a large number of Jewish subcontractors. As in Leicester, many of those whom the census returns might lead us to class under the heading of dressmakers are in reality employed by makers-up of knitted goods. At the same time there has been a genuine expansion of the wholesale dressmaking, blouse and underclothing trades during the last fifteen years, and the numbers thus employed now reach about 5000. This makes Nottingham the leading dressmaking city outside London and Manchester. The class of trade done is a high one. The heavier Mantle trade is also represented, though on a much smaller scale.

The growth of the light sewing trade, which has gone hand in hand with an expansion of the knitted wear making-up trade, is to be accounted for by the decline in the demand for machine-made lace, or " Nottingham lace," as it is commonly called. The lace manufacture is the industry, *par excellence*, for which Nottingham used to be noted, though the city has also long been known as a leading centre for engineering, cycles, drugs and chemicals, and a variety of other products. Already before the war changing tastes had brought about a decline of the lace trade, and it is now in a state of serious stagnation, which shows every sign of being permanent. The very large reserve of female labour thus created has been taken advantage of by employers in the dressmaking and making-up trades, to set up new factories for this class of work ; in addition far-sighted lace manufacturers have struck out on the new line for themselves, starting with the advantage of a staff and an organization already in existence, instead of waiting to be slowly forced out by economic forces beyond their control. The disappearance (or rather the decline, for it has not of course by any means entirely disappeared) of the lace trade is scarcely a matter for serious regret by the social reformer, as it used to share with the shirt and chain-making trades the reputation of being one of the worst sweated of all British industries. The newer firms, starting with a clean sheet in this respect, have not followed in the footsteps of their predecessors, and although they many of them give work out to home-workers, whose habitations are not all that can be desired, the wages paid are a great improvement on those current twenty years ago. Most of the credit, here as every-where, is of course due to the Trade Board legislation, but for which there is every reason to suppose that the traditions of the lace trade of the past would have been inherited by the light clothing trade of the present.

THE EASTERN COUNTIES

East Anglia is a district the importance of which as a clothing centre has declined. The industry is mainly to be found in and around Norwich, Colchester and Ipswich, where, 2000, 1700 and 1600 clothing workers respectively find employment.

Norwich does a varied trade, including several kinds of women's garments as well as some tropical wear, for which latter it is indeed the leading centre in the country. Much tropical wear, as well as low-grade export goods, is made by home-workers in the surrounding villages, as well as in Norwich itself. Ipswich is chiefly engaged in the women's trades, more especially corsets and blouses. The corset-makers form about one-third of the total number of clothing operatives in the town. Colchester, on the other hand, is exclusively a centre for men's tailoring, including, like Norwich, some tropical goods. The best known firm in the town is Hyams, which does a good class of men's trade. Many of the machinists in this factory are men, which is most unusual, and can only be accounted for by the fact that, the district being agricultural, the general level of wages is low, and men are therefore willing to enter occupations which they would elsewhere consider insufficiently paid. Apart from these three towns there is no other centre in the Eastern Counties in which the clothing industry proper is carried on on any considerable scale, though Yarmouth is noted for the manufacture of oilskins. The Census figures show a considerable number of clothing workers, especially shirt-makers in Essex, but most of these are to be found on the south-western borders of the county and may more properly be regarded as being in the Metropolitan area. A notable feature of the industry in the foregoing towns is the complete absence of Jewish labour. In this respect they do not really differ from other towns of similar size, for the Jew seems to be naturally attracted to the larger centres of population. Another point worth noticing is the almost complete absence of organization among the workers. This, also, is to be expected, since it is in the Eastern Counties that the trade union movement has usually met with the least success.

It may be inferred that it is largely the depressed wage level that is responsible for the continuance of the industry in a part of the country remote from the large industrial centres. The rapid industrialization of the southern portion of East Anglia which is now in process may possibly have far-reaching effects on the local clothing industry. On the one hand the general rise in the standard of living with which it is accompanied may drive the employees into other occupations ; on the other, the growth of population, creating a large local market, may cause the industry to expand. Perhaps the Birmingham district affords a fair comparison. Chelmsford shares with Coventry the distinction of having the lowest proportion of unemployment in the country, and in general it is largely Essex or the region south-east and east of Birmingham which such new industries as artificial silk and electrical engineering have specially chosen as their home. In the case of Birmingham, as we have seen, the clothing trades have declined, and it is possible that the relatively insignificant industry of East Anglia will suffer a similar eclipse. On the other hand, it is equally likely that the clothing trades will share in the general exodus from London to the Home Counties, which has recently been observable among industries principally dependent on electrical power. All that can be said is that no such tendency can as yet be discerned.

THE LONDON AREA

In most countries the capital city is the leading centre for the clothing trades. Not only is it normally the chief centre of population ; still more is it the centre of elegant society, whither all who can afford to do so travel periodically to visit the shops and assure themselves that they are not behind the fashion. This is true in America of New York ; it is true in France of Paris ; and equally in England is it true of London. Here in the West End are all the best tailors and costumiers and outfitters in the country, and here in the East End is a very fair proportion of the clothing factories as well. According to the latest census figures, the total number of workers in the clothing trades of the county of London is 156,233 out of a population of $4\frac{1}{2}$ millions. To this figure must be added another 20,000 living in the adjoining districts of Essex, Middlesex, Surrey, and Kent, who should properly be included

in the Metropolitan area. The figures can be further analysed
as follows :

	Men	Women	Total
Tailoring	39,999	37,951	77,950
Dress, Blouse and Millinery .	3,487	50,815	54,302
Shirts, Collars, Underclothing,			
Handkerchiefs, Ties . .	2,825	12,800	15,625
Stays and Corsets . . .	432	1,775	2,207
Hats and Caps . . .	2,868	3,281	6,149

Of the tailors probably 5000 are in the West End handicraft
trade, the remainder in the subdivisional trade, most of them
employed either by some 1600 subcontractors (not directly by
the retailers), or in the wholesale clothing factories. " Dress,
Blouse and Millinery " includes those engaged in the mantle
and the various light clothing trades, other than underclothing.

The most compact of these groups is that of the handicraft
tailors, all of whom are to be found in Central London, and
mainly in Soho. Most of them work at home, though a fair
proportion resort to hired " sittings." These are large rooms,
rented and managed by a man who is often himself a working
tailor and who sublets to several others. His tenants arrive daily
to do their work, each having his allotted place on the tailors'
bench. The rent which has to be paid for the room is generally
exorbitant, and it is not unusual for each tailor to pay 6s. a
week for his share in a room where there are perhaps a dozen
men at work. The place is usually stuffy and dirty, and in
winter is apt to be either overheated or else excessively cold.
From every point of view the " sitting " is an institution one
would like to see abolished. Only a small minority of the 5000
handicraft tailors were ever employed on what is called the
" indoor " system, that is on the premises of their employers.
This number fell even lower during the war, and now amounts
to but 5 per cent. of the whole, *i.e.* to two to three hundred.
Under this system provision is sometimes, though rarely, made

for the accommodation of the women helps who are employed and paid by the journeymen tailors themselves. The officials of the trade unions are strongly in favour of the universal adoption of " indoor " employment, though many of the rank and file undoubtedly prefer freedom to healthy surroundings. This militates against the chance of success, in any case a slender one, in the campaign for the abolition of outwork. Another obstacle lies in the fact that the structural alterations in the employers' premises which their adaptation for the " indoor " system would involve, are in by no means all cases feasible. It seems probable, therefore, that the existing arrangements will remain unchanged for some time to come. This is much to be deplored, as the conditions among the outworkers in the West End are as bad as anything to be found in the country, and are tending, as the congestion in Central London gets more acute, to deteriorate still further. Many of the outworkers now live in outlying districts, such as Shepherd's Bush and Finchley, and merely come in every day to work in the " sittings." The result of this exodus from the overcrowded region of Soho is probably to improve the living conditions of the tailors' families, but of course it entails a considerable expenditure in fares and it perpetuates the evils specially associated with the sittings.

The employers are nearly all members of the " Association of London Master Tailors," an exclusive body which only admits to its ranks firms employing none but handicraft tailors. Several of these firms, such as Pooles of Savile Row, are household names throughout the country, and indeed, as is well known, the West End has long been the Mecca of the well-dressed man, whether he hail from Cornwall or Caithness, from Paris or Chicago or Peking. All told there are slightly over a hundred firms who could qualify for the blue riband of the tailoring trade—membership of the A.L.M.T.

Of the 5000 handicraft tailors a fair proportion are foreigners, notably Swedes ; practically none are Jews, though some few women helps are Jewesses. A strong nucleus is organized, the Amalgamated Society of Tailors and Tailoresses claiming about 700 West End members and the Tailors' and Garment Workers' Trade Union about 400. Relations with the masters are fairly cordial, in spite of the widespread dissatisfaction with existing conditions of work among the men. Perhaps this is due to the common feeling of craftsmanship which animates masters and men alike, and the natural conservatism of a calling which ministers exclusively to the needs of the well-to-do. On the other hand, the two unions are constantly quarrelling among themselves, since the A.S.T. & T. takes the view that it has the right to an undisputed sway among the handicraft tailors, and regards the other union, whose West End branch is a creation of comparatively recent years, as an unwarranted intruder, while the latter claims that there ought to be only one union among clothing workers, factory operatives and handicraftsmen alike. This matter will be discussed more fully in the chapter on Trade Unionism.

More than one study of the Soho tailors has already appeared. It is thus unnecessary to describe here in detail the extreme seasonal fluctuations of demand, the high piece-rates and the low annual earnings, the peculiarly complicated system of payment known as the London log, the unhealthy conditions of the homes where the tailors do their work in the midst of their families, the female members of which often help with the easier parts of the garments, and the violent alternations of gloom and cheerfulness to which they are subject with the changing seasons. All these and other picturesque details of the lives of these " aristocrats " of the tailoring industry have been adequately described in other pages,[1] or else they are treated elsewhere in this study.

[1] *E.g.*, Barbara Drake's study in *Seasonal Trades*. Ed. Sidney Webb, London School of Economics. 1912.

Broadly speaking, there has been little change in the conditions which prevailed before the war. The most notable tendency has been the diminution in the number of handicraft tailors, the chief cause of which is undoubtedly the impossibility of attracting apprentices to so precarious and so unhealthy an occupation.[1] This seems likely to continue, and the effect has been, and will be still more so in the future, to compel even the proudest firms of all to consider the ways of their humbler but more numerous brethren who have frankly abandoned old methods of production and have introduced in varying degrees the principle of subdivisional work, and possibly to induce them to do likewise.

It is with this type of firm that all but the most fortunate of us are accustomed to have dealings, though often we mistake for the " real thing " that we should patronize if we were in a stronger financial position. It is a type of establishment which often has two or more shops in different parts of London. It is specially common in the neighbourhood of Southampton Row, Kingsway and the Strand, as well as farther east in the city. Many, though only a small proportion, of these firms belong to the National Federation of Merchant Tailors, a body which will be in greater detail described in the chapter on " Employers' Associations." In a few cases some of the work is done on the premises, though more usually, and nearly always to some extent, Jewish subcontractors are employed. We may say in passing that, though they would be loath to admit it, even some of the lordly " Master Tailors " of the Hanover Square region have on occasion adopted these methods. In fact there is no exact dividing line between the one class of trade and the other. There are many places in Kingsway or the City where a suit every bit as good as the real West End article can be obtained for somewhere about half the price of a similar production bearing a name famous in the sartorial

[1] See also below, Chapter VIII.

annals of the past two centuries. At the other end the
" Merchant Tailors " of humbler repute have their garments
made up by the better-class wholesale clothiers, in Leeds and
elsewhere, or by big Jewish subcontracting-houses in the
East End, where the subdivisional system has been so elaborated
as to differ in no essential respect from ordinary factory
methods. In so doing they are copying the large department
stores, such as Selfridge's, Harrod's and Barker's, which, in
addition to stocking a large range of ready-mades or " ready-
to-wears," [1] do a brisk trade in made-to-measure clothes, which
they have made by the same firms. One such firm of subcontractors employs some 700 work-people, thus rivalling in
size all but the largest wholesale factories, while there are
several whose employees number anything from 80 to 100 or
more. Firms of this size cut the garments as well as making
them ; the smaller subcontractors, with teams of a dozen or
twenty, receive the material from the Merchant Tailor ready
cut, and are only concerned with the making of it into
clothes.

A great many of these subcontractors are in the East End,
especially in Whitechapel, or at any rate outside Central
London ; there are, however, a fair number in the Tottenham
Court Road district and even in Soho itself, the home of the
English handicraft tailor. In most cases these West End subcontractors have rather smaller teams than those suggested
above. Nearly always the Jewish master of a small business
works side by side with his men. Wages are good, but the
standard of efficiency set is a high one. and the slow or in-

---

[1] A ready-to-wear garment is not so completely finished as an
ordinary ready-made, and can be altered quite considerably to suit the
individual customer. It first attained popularity among well-dressed
men during the war, when clothes were often required almost at a
moment's notice. Since then the department stores have developed it
into quite a speciality. Though the fit is naturally not as perfect as
that of a specially-cut suit, these clothes command a ready sale at prices
up to £9, 9s. or £10, 10s. a suit.

competent worker meets with little sympathy. The workshops
are apt to be crowded and under-ventilated, and the hours
long and irregular. The fact that many tailoring firms look
on the subcontractor as a person to be resorted to only in
moments of emergency means that an undue proportion of
the burden of seasonal fluctuations finds its way on to his
shoulders. Ground also between the upper millstone of a
rapacious employer and the nether millstone of a staff determined to maintain wages at a high level, he sometimes finds
himself left with a very small margin of profit on turnover.
This was demonstrated many years ago by Mrs. Webb, who
destroyed the illusion of a bloated subcontractor strolling up
and down in his " sweater's den " in a fur coat and smoking
a fat cigar, an illusion which had found currency in the Press
and in the cartoons of *Punch*. It is sometimes even the case
that the so-called sweater finds his net weekly profit is less
than the wage he has to pay to the best of his workmen,
though of course he has the consolation, no small one to the
average Jew, of being an employer and not a hired hand.
Such instances are at the same time comparatively rare, and
the long hours worked and the tremendous industry characteristic of the subdivisional tailor or tailoress, enable a
handsome profit to be earned at a low rate on turnover.

The subcontractors are organized in yet another employers'
association—" The Master Tailors' Association." This, like
the " National Federation of Merchant Tailors," is a nation-
wide body, but its principal strength lies in London, where it
boasts 600 members. It is in no way connected with the
" Association of London Master Tailors," the similarity of
title being due to the fact that the subcontractors have called
themselves by the same name as the very different proprietors
of retail tailoring establishments of the West End. As we
shall see when we come to discuss the Trade Boards, this
Association sometimes finds itself in an anomalous position,

feeling sympathy with the workers when the discussion ranges round the price a retail tailor should pay for the making of a suit, and with the employers when it turns to a consideration of actual time- or piece-rates, or of general conditions of employment.

Before turning to the wholesale trades in London, we may note that it is not men's clothing alone which is made directly by retail firms. A very large number of mantles and gowns, dresses, blouses, jumpers and even underclothes, as well as millinery of all kinds, are made in the workshops of department stores and drapers and fashionable modistes. These establishments vary considerably in the treatment they accord to their employees, some of the best being exceptionally generous. The old habit of " living in " has much diminished, though several firms, among whom we may mention Messrs. Bourne and Hollinsworth, provide large hostels for their employees, where comfortable accommodation can be obtained at very reasonable rates. In these cases no compulsion is brought to bear on employees to avail themselves of the facilities provided, but there is often keen competition for the privilege. In view of the increasing difficulty in finding lodgings in or near Central London, one of the chief advantages of this provision is a considerable saving of time and money which would otherwise be spent on the daily journey to and from home. In a few firms, of which Jay's at Oxford Circus affords an example, some of the employees still live actually on the premises in the upper floors, but the high level of rents in important shopping thoroughfares makes this very rare. Much of the credit for the recent improvement in the lot of the employees is due to the " London Employers' Association," an organization which was formed in 1918 and which comprises many, but by no means all, of the firms engaged in the women's clothing trade, especially the larger ones. The primary object of the Association is to form agreements with the Clothing Unions, though it also fulfils most of the usual functions of an employers' organization, preparing special reports about trade conditions, studying problems of recruitment, etc. It has come to a series of agreements with the principal unions, including the Shop Assistants and the General Workers, regulating conditions of employment, fixing wage-rates at a level in some cases higher than that imposed by the Trade Boards, and making provision for meal-times, overtime, annual holidays, and a variety of other matters. We shall discuss its activities at greater length in another chapter.

Turning now to the wholesale trades, we find them being carried on in almost every quarter of the metropolis, though there are certain districts where they tend to congregate in specially large numbers.

First there is a small district in Central London, mainly north and east of Oxford Circus. We have already noted the existence of a large number of Jewish subcontractors in this neighbourhood, who work for the West End tailors, but there are also several costume, mantle and blouse firms, small establishments for the most part, also frequently owned by Jews.

In the East End the district which stands out above all others is Whitechapel and the adjoining parishes. Aldgate East, Houndsditch, the Minories, Commercial Road, Norton Folgate, Middlesex Street and the neighbouring thoroughfares are inhabited mainly by Jewish clothing workers in one line of business or another. As we proceed farther east to Poplar and Limehouse we pass every now and then a clothing factory of some description. In Limehouse there is a wholesale tailoring and a shirt and pyjama firm, in the East India Dock Road a firm specializing in engineers' overalls, in Barking Road a firm of government clothing manufacturers, while Dockland, generally speaking, boasts a number of factories mainly engaged in the production of low-grade garments. It is on the earnings of the women here employed that many a dock-labourer's family depends for its regular means of subsistence, while the nominal head of the family hangs about the docks waiting for jobs which are only intermittent.

Next to Whitechapel in importance is Clerkenwell. This is essentially a district of miscellaneous minor industries, chief among which are boots and clothing. In Old Street and City Road are wholesale tailoring, mantle, raincoat, blouse and underclothing, juvenile and other clothing manufacturers, as well as firms engaged in such kindred trades as fur, fancy feather, art needlework and artificial flowers. The number of Jews employed is large, but they do not here enjoy the monopoly which they do in Whitechapel.

Other centres of some importance are Bethnal Green, Clapton, Islington, Stoke Newington, and Hackney. Near the latter is Old Ford, where there is a famous firm of uniform clothing contractors—Messrs. Compton as well as one or two other wholesale clothiers. Walthamstow is worth mentioning as a centre for shirts and pyjamas and for women's light clothing. In South London the only district in which the clothing industry is highly localized is New Cross, which does a similar trade to Walthamstow. We may also notice Woolwich on the south-east and Southwark. In the western suburbs Shepherd's Bush takes the lead, while light dressmaking establishments are to be found in Richmond, Willesden, and elsewhere.

It may be noted that in the East End it is the higher classes of the clothing trades in which the Jews are mainly engaged. In Whitechapel, in particular, some of the very best wholesale bespoke tailoring in the country is to be found. The Gentiles engaged in the clothing trades, on the other hand, often come from some of the lower strata of society, as in the case of the dockers' women-folk, to whom we have already alluded. It is only in Whitechapel that a considerable proportion of the population is engaged in making clothes, and it must have been to this district that a writer in the May 1921 number of *The Garment Worker* was referring when he stated that " about half the women in some parts of the East End are engaged in some part of the trade."

The East End workers are badly organized. The Tailors' and Garment Workers' Trade Union maintains a full-time staff and an office in Norton Folgate. A fair proportion of the wholesale tailoring operatives has been enrolled, and it may even be said that some factories are " closed shops," but in other sections of the trade the number of trade unionists is negligible. This is, no doubt, largely because many factories making women's clothes employ no male labour at all, not even pressers, and it is nearly always through the male employees that the women get organized. The East End cutters, unlike their more aristocratic West End brethren, who normally look on life from the employers' point of view, are mostly members of the Union, and it is they, more than anyone, who have been successful in getting some of the girls in the factories where they themselves are employed to join up.

As in the case of the West End tailors of Soho, a detailed description of the different types of clothing workers in East London is superfluous, because it has been so frequently given before. Minor changes in the outer semblance of their lives have taken place since the publication of the study of East London, carried out in the 80's by Charles Booth and his collaborators, but the broad outlines are unchanged. The most notable difference is the fall in the number of outworkers and the improvement in the condition of those still employed. How many there yet remain it is difficult to estimate, certainly several thousands working for low-grade tailoring firms, for a small number of Jewish subcontractors in the tailoring and mantle trades, and for manufacturers of light clothing, underclothing, and, particularly, shirts. In spite of the difficulties which would attend its complete extinction, it is much to be hoped that this goal will in time be achieved. The steady extension of the ready-made trade, the gradual growth in the power of the Garment Workers' Union, and the increasing efficiency with which the Trade Board and other Governmental regulations are enforced, may ultimately lead to this result.

SCOTLAND

The number of clothing workers of all kinds in Scotland is 88,000. Of these the city of Glasgow claims 24,000 and the neighbouring county of Lanark 35,000. Edinburgh comes a bad third with 9000.

In the Census figures those engaged in " Tailoring " (which includes mantle manufacturing) are numbered at 21,041, mainly in the above three districts, and in " Dressmaking, etc." at 49,563, also mainly in the above districts, together with a fair contingent from Aberdeen. Practically all other clothing trades — caps, shirts, corsets, handkerchiefs and underclothing generally—are confined to Glasgow.

In retail tailoring Edinburgh enjoys the highest reputation in the country for style and fit, while in point of numbers it is only beaten by a short head by Glasgow, the respective figures being 1100 and 1400. Some of the Edinburgh firms, indeed, rank with the most famous in the West End of London, and find a numerous clientele in the landed gentry who form a relatively larger proportion of the population of Scotland than of England. In the less important towns, and even in quite small villages, handicraft tailors are still to be found in considerable numbers, and a notable fact concerning them is that almost every one is a member of his local trade union branch. Except in the places where the A.S.T. & T. has a foothold (*i.e.* Dundee, Forfar, Aberdeen and Glasgow), a list of the handicraft branches of the Garment Workers' Union in Scotland is thus a fairly reliable guide to the numbers of tailors in each locality.

Jewish subcontractors are scarce except in Glasgow, where they are more numerous than in any other centre but London. Their methods and the conditions under which they work are in no way different from those prevailing in London and elsewhere, and do not call for special comment.

As we have seen, Glasgow and the neighbourhood engages in a considerable variety of trades in the factory group. Chief among these are men's tailoring and mantles, though in many cases what would appear from a Trades Directory to be clothing factories are in reality warehouses belonging to firms in Leeds, London, and elsewhere, and serving as distributing centres for the Scottish market, possibly engaging also on a limited scale in the export trade. Such, for instance, is the Glasgow branch of Messrs. Gerrish, Ames & Simpkins, the well-known clothiers and warehousemen of London and Basingstoke. In other cases firms whose head offices are at Glasgow do not actually manufacture locally, but have factories situated elsewhere, especially in Leeds.

The shirt trade is a considerable one, the Glasgow district ranking as one of the principal centres outside Northern Ireland. Some firms own factories both in Glasgow and in Derry or the neighbourhood. For caps Glasgow is also of considerable importance, and this trade it shares with Manchester, Stockport and London. There are several underclothing factories, one or two in the blouse and the baby-linen trade, and one at least in the skirt and costume and the handkerchief trade. Corsets are principally made on a retail scale by people in quite a small way of business.

Glasgow has in the past shared the bad reputation for sweated outwork in the clothing trades which has been common in most large towns where the industry is located. The slums

F

of Glasgow are notorious for their narrow and dirty streets and for the tall and barrack-like tenement houses with which they are lined. In these houses, in many a squalid bedroom-cum-workshop, shirts and blouses and underclothes used to be made, and outer garments of all sorts used to be finished, often under insanitary conditions which endangered the health of the prospective wearer as well as of the maker of the clothes. Much of this homework has now been transferred to the factories, and the conditions under which such as still remain is performed have improved. As everywhere in the case of homework, exact figures are impossible to obtain.

CHAPTER IV

WAGE REGULATION AND THE TRADE BOARDS

THE principal machinery for wage regulation in the clothing industry since 1919 has been the Trade Boards system. Except in the case of handicraft tailoring, where collective bargaining has been in operation for many years, there was until 1909 no regular method of adjusting wages in any section of the industry. In that year the first Trade Board was set up, for the Wholesale Tailoring trade ; but it was not until after the war that, largely on the strength of the reports of the Whitley Committee on Industrial Relations, which recommended that machinery for the compulsory enforcement of minimum wage-rates on Trade Board lines should be applied to all industries where the workers and employers are insufficiently organized to render collective bargaining of the ordinary type (or even Joint Industrial Committees) effective, the Trade Board system was applied to all sections of the clothing trades.

It will be pointed out in Chapter V that cases frequently occur where collective agreements outside the scope of the Trade Board system have been arrived at, often embodying rates more favourable to the workers than those enforced by the Boards. None the less, since these are the exception rather than the rule, we shall here confine our attention to the composition and activities of the Trade Boards. It has become abundantly clear that the hope expressed in the Whitley Committee's reports that they would afford a mere stepping-stone on the way to unfettered collective bargaining is unlikely to be realized at least for many years to come.

The Boards (which consist of employers and workers in equal numbers, appointed by the Minister of Labour, as far as possible on the nomination of representative bodies of the two parties, together with a certain number, normally three, of eminent outsiders, known as " Appointed Members," selected directly by the Minister) have as their almost exclusive function the settlement of minimum rates in the industries they represent. They are at liberty to recommend any rates they think fit, which, after being ratified by the Minister of Labour, become legally enforceable. The actual enforcement of the rates is no direct concern of the Boards, but rests with the Ministry, which maintains a special body of inspectors for the purpose and prosecutes recalcitrant employers. The control of this inspectorate, together with all matters relating to the formation and working of the Boards, is in the hands of a separate department of the Ministry, known as the Office of Trade Boards. In connection with the enforcement of Minimum Rates, the Minister of Labour has power under the Trade Boards Acts to require the posting, in all premises coming within the scope of the Acts, of notices of minimum rates ; the keeping by employers of adequate records of rates paid and time worked ; and the observance of sundry other incidental regulations, failure to comply with which may likewise lead to prosecution.

It forms no part of this report to deal in any but a general way with the establishment and early history of the Boards. This task has been adequately performed in earlier publications of the Ratan Tata Foundation,[1] as well as in the official " Report to the Minister of Labour of the Committee appointed to enquire into the Working and Effects of the Trade Boards

---

[1] See bibliography on pp. 203-4. See also Bulkley, M. E. The Establishment of Minimum Rates in the Box Making Industry under the Trade Boards Act, 1909. The Ratan Tata Foundation (University of London). Studies in the Minimum Wage, No. III.

Acts." [The Cave Committee (Cmd. 1645), 1922.] At the same
time, a very short summary of the main lines of development
on which the Trade Board system as applied to the clothing
trades has proceeded will serve to throw some light on the
position it now occupies.

Among the sweated industries, the conditions prevalent in
which it was the object of the framers of the Boards to remedy,
" Ready-made and Wholesale Bespoke Tailoring " takes the
first place, whether it be regarded from the point of view of the
number of workers engaged, the annual value of the product,
or the importance of industry in the national life. The other
three industries to which the Trade Boards Act of 1909 was at
first applied were the Paper-box Trade, the Machine-made
Lace Trade and the Chain-making Trade. It had originally
been proposed that Shirt-making, in which the existence of
much underpaid homework had been revealed by the Homework enquiries of 1907 and 1908, should be included in the list,
but Chain-making was substituted at the last moment. After
a few years' experience had shown how efficacious the Act had
been in achieving the ends at which it aimed, Shirt-making
was included by a Provisional Order of the Board of Trade in
1914, two separate Boards, one for Great Britain and the other
for Ireland, being established.[1]

No further extensions of the system took place till after the
passing of the Trade Boards Act of 1918. Under this Act, based
largely on the Reports of the Whitley Committee, provision
was made for the establishment of Trade Boards not only, as
theretofore, in trades in which wages were excessively low,
but also where, to some extent irrespectively of the actual
wage rates prevailing, organization amongst employees or
workers was excessively weak. This made it possible to deal
with a large number of trades without attaching to them the

[1] Boards were also established in 1914 for the Sugar Confectionery,
etc., the Tin-box and the Hollow-ware trades.

stigma of being " sweated trades," and thus without running so much danger of antagonizing employers. Amongst other classes of workers thus brought within the jurisdiction of the Trade Boards, the entire body of clothing workers not already provided for now found a place. These included all the workers in the women's trades, together with tailors working on handicraft lines for retail bespoke firms. In point of fact many of these would no doubt have been eligible for inclusion under the earlier Act. They had been omitted for a variety of reasons. In the first place, the 1909 Act was admittedly experimental, and was only applied to a few of the trades where " sweating " was known to exist. Secondly, in the case of retail tailoring, the authorities were to some extent deceived by the high rates of hourly wages which have always been a characteristic of this section of the industry. In the wholesale section, especially in districts where homework prevailed extensively, the industry was notorious for the low rates of wages. In the retail section, the lowest rates were paid in some of the south coast and south-western towns, particularly naval towns like Portsmouth and Plymouth. But even there the wages *per hour* were relatively high. What was overlooked was the extent to which seasonal unemployment reduced annual earnings. This gradually became more evident, especially when the necessity for raising wages owing to rising war-time prices led to comparisons between one industry and another. Thirdly, in the women's section of the industry, while there was no doubt about the fact that organization was practically non-existent, it was not clear to what extent wages were unduly low. Some branches, such as retail millinery and high-class dressmaking, have always been well remunerated, others very poorly. But the greater complexity of the women's trades made demarcation exceedingly difficult ; this was found to be true even after the war, when several years' experience in dealing with wage-problems in other branches of industry, and the considerable development of organization on both sides during the war, made the task of establishing suitable Trade Boards in the women's trades considerably easier than it would have been in 1914.

The first step taken with regard to the clothing trades under the new Act was to apply it to retail bespoke tailoring. This was done partly for the reason above-mentioned, that annual earnings were much below what they appeared to be on the surface, and partly because it was increasingly felt that the distinction between wholesale bespoke and retail bespoke methods was a difficult one to draw in practice, that nearly all tailors were now employing subdivisional methods to some extent, and that accordingly, while it might be reasonable to establish a separate Board for the retail bespoke trade, it would be clearly unfair to maintain any longer the dwindling body of genuine retail bespoke tailors as a privileged class of employees excluded from the working of the Trade Boards Acts. Accordingly the old Tailoring Trade Board was dissolved and two new Boards were established, the Retail Bespoke Tailoring Board (Great Britain) on 12th December 1919, and the Ready-made and Wholesale Bespoke Board (Great Britain) on 17th February 1920. Two similar Boards were established for Ireland on 24th April 1920. In the first of these Boards the predominant parties on the workers' side have been the Amalgamated Society of Tailors and Tailoresses and the United Garment Workers' Trade Union ; on the employers' side the National Federation of Merchant Tailors, which at first supplied ten out of twenty employers' representatives, and the Association of London Master Tailors. In the Wholesale Tailoring Board the workers are mainly represented by the U.G.W.T.U. and the employers by the Wholesale Clothiers Federation, but other bodies, such as the London Employers' Association, are also represented. On this Board the Jewish Master Tailors sit on the employers' side, as they do on that of the Wholesale Mantle and Costume Board. As has been indicated previously, this places them at times in a doubtful and unenviable position, in which their interests as subcontractors and their interests as employers are often at variance.

In the case of the Trade Boards for the women's trades the initial difficulties chiefly arose in deciding how many Boards should be established, and what sections of the industry each should cover. In the first place, the idea of including the mantle trade with men's tailoring, which had at first been entertained, owing to the general similarity of the two occupations, was abandoned in response to the representations of the mantle manufacturers. In accordance with this decision the Wholesale Mantle and Costume Trade Board (Great Britain) was established on 13th December 1919, and a similar Board for Ireland on 31st March 1920. On this Board the United Garment Workers' Trade Union supplied the bulk of the workers' representatives, while employers were drawn from a great variety of towns and sections of the trade, including the big London stores, the wholesale houses, the subcontractors, the raincoat trade, and others.

The wholesale mantle trade was one which it was comparatively easy to deal with as a single whole. When it came to the other women's trades demarcation difficulties became almost insuperable. The Drapers' Chamber of Commerce, for instance, pressed for the establishment of one Board to cover Retail Dressmaking and Millinery and another for Wholesale Dressmaking and Millinery. No sooner had this suggestion been put forward than practical difficulties in carrying it out presented themselves. Originally millinery had been an almost entirely retail trade, but this is no longer the case. For some time past shapes for hats have been made by wholesale firms in Luton and sold to retailers, who trim them and sell them. In many cases nowadays, where the trimming required is only a bit of ribbon or a bow, the complete hat is made at

Luton and bought by the retailer ready for sale. On the other hand, many London drapers make their own hats, and in this case the question whether they are retailers or wholesalers depends largely on the size of their turnover. The position is still further complicated by the fact that some firms dispose of their product partly by selling direct to the public and partly by selling to other smaller retailers. In the end it was decided that a single Board should be established to cover the Hat, Cap and Millinery trade, whether retail or wholesale, and that the rest of the women's trades should be lumped together under the title of Dressmaking and Women's Light Clothing, this title to include the retail Mantle trade, together with the wholesale and retail manufacture of Light Outer Clothing, and Underclothing. Separate Boards in each case were established for England and Wales, for Scotland and for Ireland, the actual dates of establishment being as follows :

12th Jan. 1920. Hat, Cap and Millinery. (England and Wales.)

15th Jan. 1920. Dressmaking and Women's Light Clothing. (England and Wales.)

29th Mar. 1920. Dressmaking and Women's Light Clothing. (Scotland.)

31st Mar. 1920. Dressmaking and Women's Light Clothing. (Ireland.)

31st Mar. 1920. Hat, Cap and Millinery. (Scotland.)

31st Mar. 1920. Hat, Cap and Millinery. (Ireland.)

There is also a Corset Trade Board and a Fur Trade Board.

On most of these Boards the Tailors' and Garment Workers' Trade Union supplies most of the workers' representatives for England and Wales. In the case of the Shirt Board, it was the circumstance that members of the T. & G.W.T.U. came into contact with representatives of the Shirtmakers' Trade Union at meetings of the Trade Board, which led to the eventual amalgamation of the latter union with the former. In the case of the Scottish Boards the Scottish branch of the Shop Assistants' Union is well represented. Employers are drawn from many different sources. It is not the practice of the Ministry of Labour to publish details of the various bodies invited to nominate members of the Boards, as it is felt to be important that members should be regarded as representatives of the trade as a whole and in no sense of any particular organization. As such they are expected to act not as delegates with instructions to carry out, but as independent members of a body responsible to no one but itself and to the Minister of Labour. It need hardly be added that this view of the situation is not always shared by the nominating bodies. A further objection to the publication of details is that such a procedure would lead to unnecessary jealousy and recriminations from bodies not called upon to furnish nominations, or which consider themselves under-represented.

The number and demarcation of the Boards has remained unchanged, with the exception that, after repeated demands from a variety of quarters, the Retail Bespoke Board was split up early in 1925, two new Boards being constituted to replace it, one for England and Wales on 20th January 1925, and the other for Scotland on the 29th February 1925. Conditions affecting the trade differ considerably in Scotland from those south of the border. The Scottish " log " has certain special features ; the Scottish tailor has a very strongly defined individual point of view; and whereas in England the workers are nearly all members of the A.S.T. & T., in Scotland they belong to the T. & G.W.T.U. It may be added that in Scotland the process of displacement of the handicraft tailors by subdivisional and factory workers has not proceeded at anything like the same pace as it has in England. It will be seen that there are now separate Boards for Scotland (as well as, of course, for Ireland) in all branches of the Clothing Trades, except Mantles and Wholesale Tailoring. From the first the retailers in Scotland were insistent that they should be allotted special Boards. A large number of the Scottish workers in the women's trades are in the Scottish branch of the Shop Assistants' Union, and this affords an additional reason for separation from the trade in England, where very few of the workers are organized at all. In the case of mantles and wholesale tailoring, the trade in Scotland is so small that separate representation would hardly be justified.

The size of the Boards varies very considerably. The largest Clothing Board is the Hat, Cap and Millinery Board (England and Wales), with 61 members, and the smallest the Retail Bespoke Tailoring Board (Scotland), with 21. It has been suggested that bodies of this size are unwieldy, and also that they entail an unnecessary expenditure of public funds and loss of time on the part of both employers and workers. While the latter objection is undoubtedly of some importance, it is difficult to see how adequate representation of all the interests involved could be secured with a smaller membership, and the former objection has not been so evident in practice as it would sound in theory. In many cases the objections have evidently been made by people opposed root and branch to the Trade Board system ; for those who have been loudest in their condemnation of the size of the Boards have also been most anxious to secure the appointment of District Committees, which obviously involve a further expenditure, both of time and money.

In each case there are three members nominated by the Ministry of Labour known as " Appointed Members," and not representing either workers or employers. At one time the number of the Appointed Members on the Retail Bespoke Tailoring Board was larger, but the opportunity to reduce it was taken when the Board was split up to form the English and Scottish Boards, on each of which there are now three

" Appointed Members." These are drawn from the learned professions, particularly the law and the Universities, and from the ranks of men and women who are well known for their interest in social and industrial problems, without being definitely associated with particular bodies. In several cases the same individual sits on several Boards, and this is especially noticeable in the case of the Hat, Cap and Millinery, and the Dressmaking and Women's Light Clothing Boards. In addition, the Chairman of two Boards (for England) is also Chairman of the Ready-made and Wholesale Bespoke Board for Great Britain. At times the policy of selecting the same individual to serve on several Boards has also been followed in the case of the workers' representatives, some of whom are drawn from the class of social workers which furnishes many of the " Appointed Members." This principle is adopted in the case of men or women who have been so closely interested in the fortunes of the Trade Union movement that they would be looked upon by the employers' representatives with suspicion if they sat as " Appointed Members." While open complaints about " the ignorance," " the bias " and " the academic uselessness " of the Appointed Members are at times to be heard in after-dinner speeches, and in the files of the Employers' Associations' publications, the value of their work is very real and is readily admitted by the better type of employer. They are especially useful in co-ordinating the policies of the different Boards, and in acting as peacemakers between the two sides when an apparent *impasse* is reached. On many occasions, in fact, they have really had to frame the decision of the Board as a whole by suggesting a middle course and enlisting the support of one or other of the two sides in conjunction with whom they have been able to outvote the other side.

During the first two years of the existence of the new Boards, their activities met with general approval. The absence of

the criticisms which might reasonably have been expected
was no doubt due partly to the widespread hope and belief
that a new and better world "fit for heroes to live in"
was going to be the first fruits of the war, partly to the
obvious necessity for some sort of authoritative machinery
for settling wages during the chaotic period of demobili-
zation and economic readjustment and partly to the fact
that, since prices continued to rise rapidly after the ter-
mination of hostilities, the wages fixed by the Boards at no
time until the end of 1921 pressed at all heavily on the
employers.[1]

When the depression of 1921 set in, the tone of the employers
immediately underwent a considerable alteration, and criticisms flowed in from every side. These related principally to
the Retail Bespoke Tailoring Board. The Wholesale Tailoring
Board and the Shirt Board had been functioning satisfactorily
since before the war, and had come to be regarded as established
institutions. The Boards dealing with the women's trades
met with comparatively little opposition, partly because the
employers in these trades were so disorganized and so hetero-
geneous that they seldom met together for consultation and
the formulation of definite criticisms, partly because a large
number of them were people in a small way of business who,
though they may have been dissatisfied, had no means of
venting their feelings in public, but chiefly perhaps because
the larger and better employers who already paid their work-
people well and treated them considerately were only too
pleased to have an effective means at their disposal of pre-
venting unscrupulous competitors from paying lower wages
and being thus enabled to sell at lower prices. Such, for
instance, was the attitude adopted by the members of the

[1] Except, that is, the wages fixed for learners and apprentices which
were objected to from the first on the ground that they were higher than
what it was worth the employers' while to pay. These were later considerably reduced. See Chapter VIII.

London Employers' Association, by far the most powerful body of employers in any of these trades.

The principal criticisms directed against the Trade Board system in general and the Retail Tailoring Trade Board in particular were as follows :

1. The Amending Act of 1918 establishing Trade Boards throughout the clothing industry was objected to. It was claimed that collective bargaining should be " restored," and that Trade Board rates should be so low as to make them *minimum* rates in the true sense of the word, and not representative rates.

2. The " Appointed Members " were objected to on the ground that their presence created an atmosphere of antagonism inside the Trade Board. It was said that if they acted in anything but an advisory capacity, and were allowed to vote, they became in effect arbitrators in matters of which they had no technical knowledge.

3. The pluralistic members of the Boards were accused of playing off one Board against another and so endangering the possibility of peaceful trade settlements.

4. The Boards were said to be unrepresentative, particularly on the workers' sides, which were composed almost exclusively of Trade Union officials and contained too few *rural* workers.

5. The regulations were described as slow-moving and cumbersome, and the procedure for varying wage-rates altogether too protracted for a highly-seasonal industry.

6. Apprentices' and learners' rates were felt to be too high.

7. The administration of the Acts was stated to be incomplete and ineffective and to fall most hardly on the best type of employer, while the really bad master succeeded in evading the law.

Other criticisms were also made, but these were the outstanding ones. We will deal with them very briefly one by one :

1. While the strength of the Trade Unions and of the Employers' Associations was much greater after than before the war, it could scarcely be claimed that in the majority of cases anything like effective machinery for collective bargaining has ever been established in the bulk of the clothing trades. Even in the case of Retail Tailoring it only exists in specially favoured districts, such as the West End of London. The case for the universal application of some governmental machinery for wage-regulation is overwhelming. It is equally clear that to establish rates which would be no higher than the *minimum* which would prevail without any intervention would be entirely nugatory. The whole purpose of the Boards is gradually to improve the general standard up to the level prevailing in well-organized industries. Exactly where this level lies is the difficult problem which it is the business of the Boards to solve.

2. While the " Appointed Members " are not technical experts, they are invariably people of proved administrative and intellectual capacity, accustomed to the task of drawing reasonable conclusions from conflicting evidence and of steering a middle course between partisan views. The fact that they are unpopular with extremists on either side is no proof of their unsuitability for the rôle they are called upon to play, but rather the reverse.

3. The principle of having pluralistic members, who form only a small minority on any of the Boards, is one of the most valuable features of the whole system. Only in this way can any sort of uniformity between the decisions of the different Boards be arrived at. Whether there are any deliberate mischief-makers among the existing pluralistic members it is,

of course, impossible for any outsider to judge, but the names of those familiar to the public are certainly not such as to inspire distrust.   The phrase " mischief-maker " is, however, one which connotes different things to different people.

4. The difficulties of securing fair representation in a very badly organized trade is admittedly considerable.   Under the circumstances it has perhaps been impossible not to rely for nominations mainly on such organizations as exist, even when these only embrace a small part of the personnel of the trade. It must also be remembered that the rural workers, while they have their own special interests, are numerically very few compared with the great masses in the big industrial centres.

5. This criticism is a fair one, and was particularly pertinent at the time it was made, when prices were moving with astounding rapidity and a corresponding elasticity in wage-rates was called for.   Something has since been done to remedy matters, and now that comparative stability has been attained, it is of considerably less importance than it was in 1921.

6. The uneconomic level at which apprentices' and learners' rates were first established by the Trade Boards was perhaps their most serious mistake.   This has now been changed.[1]

7. This criticism of the system is also a very serious one. At the same time, it is one which comes most properly from those who approve of the Trade Boards in principle rather than those who wish to see them abolished.   The whole matter is bound up with the question of expense, since the maintenance of an adequate inspectorate is bound to be a costly business. It will be discussed a little later in the present chapter.

There was undoubtedly sufficient substance in the above and similar criticisms to warrant the appointment of a " Committee of Enquiry into the Working and Effects of the Trade Boards Acts," a step which would in any case have been desirable a

[1] See Chapter VIII.

few years after the inauguration of this important and hitherto untried piece of administrative machinery. The Committee was duly appointed in 1921 under the chairmanship of Lord Cave and issued its Report, together with very voluminous minutes of evidence, in 1922. This evidence affords the chief source of information on which any critic of the Trade Board system must draw.

The Report of the Committee proved, on the whole, to be a dash of cold water for the opponents of the Trade Board system. The names of the persons appointed to serve on it had given rise in some quarters to the expectation that it would condemn the system root and branch, but in point of fact the recommendations made were by no means so drastic. Since they have been repeatedly set forth in publications dealing with industrial and social problems during the past few years,[1] only the barest summary of them need here be included.

Summary of Recommendations made by the Cave Committee.

1. Power to establish Trade Boards should be given only when a trade is shown to be one where (*a*) unduly low wages are paid, *and* (*b*) insufficient machinery for collective bargaining exists. (The 1918 Act had authorized the establishment of Boards where *either* of these conditions was fulfilled.)

2. A *public* enquiry should be held before a Trade Board is established (instead of a private enquiry by the Minister of Labour).

3. The only statutory duty of a Board should be to fix a general minimum time-rate for the *lowest grade of ordinary workers*. Boards should be allowed, but not compelled to set up other rates (such as *e.g.* General Minimum Piece-rates).

4. Boards established in manufacturing and productive

[1] See *e.g. The British Trade Board System.* Dorothy Sells. pp. 282-285.

G

trades should be encouraged to set up further District Committees,[1] without autonomous powers, to report to the Boards on matters affecting local interests.

5. In the case of distributive and retail making-up trades, the country should be divided into suitable districts in which autonomous District Boards should be set up in place of the existing National Boards. If it were considered advisable, a Central Committee should also be appointed for each of these trades to co-ordinate the decisions of the District Boards.

6. Learners' rates should take account of *experience* as well as age, and provide facilities for late entrants.

7. Apprenticeship rates on a substantially lower scale than Learners' rates should be encouraged.

8. Easier facilities for granting exemption permits for partially incapacitated workers should be available.

9. Facilities should exist for winding-up Trade Boards where the Minister thinks this advisable.

10. Daily overtime rates should only have to be paid conditionally on a minimum week's work.[2]

11. There should be greater speed in making variations of rates.

12. Employers should *at once* be warned in case of non-compliance with the official rates (instead of being allowed to go on until prosecuted).

13. A Consolidating Act should be passed to replace the existing legislation.

It will be seen that, with the exception of the first, these proposals were of comparatively secondary importance. In

---

[1] Boards have always had powers to set up such District Committees, but have not very frequently made use of them (*vide infra*, p. 100).

[2] Under existing conditions some Boards have ruled that overtime rates must be paid for all hours over 9 daily and/or over 48 weekly. See also Chapter V.

making the first the Committee sought to apply the conditions required by the Act of 1918 *as well as* and not *instead of* those required by the Act of 1909 as a preliminary to the setting up of Trade Boards.   At first sight this would appear to be an attempt to cut at the roots of the whole system ; but, as it was only intended to be a condition for the setting up of future Trade Boards, and not an engine for the dissolution of those already established, it was quite innocuous.   In point of fact the Trade Boards Act has not been applied since the Committee's Report to any fresh trades, a circumstance to be attributed as much to the wide scope of the system as it already existed in 1922 as to meticulous respect for the Committee's recommendations.[1]

A Bill to amend and consolidate the law relating to Trade Boards, embodying substantially the recommendation of the Cave Committee, was introduced by the Minister of Labour in May 1923.   Though this Bill might have been expected to meet with the approval of the employers, it failed to do so, the following Memorandum being one of the protests drawn up against it by members of the Tailoring trade.

Memorandum relating to the Trade Boards Bill 1923.[2]

1. The Minister has too much power over the Boards.

2. Time-rates should apply to the " lowest grade of worker," and not merely the " lowest grade of *fully experienced workers of ordinary skill, other than those engaged in ancillary work.*"

3. Objection is taken to the clause providing that a worker " is to be dealt with as having been employed during waiting

---

[1] It is not intended to suggest that there are no further trades whatever to which it would not be desirable to apply the Trade Boards Acts. On the contrary, the writer is in agreement with the views expressed on this subject in the Report of the Liberal Industrial Enquiry, 1928 (see p. 210 of the Report).

[2] Quoted in the *Merchant Tailor*, October 1923.

time on the employer's premises, if he has been caused to wait by the employer's express or implied representation that he will be given work that day if it becomes available for him."

4. Objection is taken to the liability of overcontractors in respect of workers employed by subcontractors, unless they are employed on the overcontractor's premises.

5. Objection is *really* taken to the existence of a Trade Board for Retail Bespoke Tailoring at all. An enquiry to determine if it is necessary should be held.

These and similar complaints so hindered the passage of the Bill that it was finally not proceeded with. Several of the recommendations of the Cave Committee were such as could be acted on by the Minister of Labour or the Boards themselves without legislative sanction, and in many cases this has been done. In particular the recommendations with regard to Learners' and Apprentices' rates have now become less necessary, and some progress in the direction of decentralization has been made.

In the Clothing Trades, District Committees had already, at the time of the Cave Committee's sittings, been established for the Shirt Board and the Retail Tailoring Board (England and Wales), and these are still functioning.[1] In the former case there are four districts and in the latter fourteen, corresponding to the fourteen districts which the National Federation of Merchant Tailors has adopted in establishing its organization. There is no doubt that these Committees have justified their existence. Local conditions in the retail tailoring trade vary enormously, both with regard to the methods of work prevailing, the class of trade done, the basis of wage payment, the cost of living, and other matters, and some measure of de-

---

[1] The Wholesale Tailoring Board at one time set up District Committees, but these appeared to serve no useful purpose (owing to the "united front" in all districts displayed by both sides), and were, therefore, discontinued.

centralization was urgently called for. It is absurd to apply exactly the same regulation to the West End of London and to Oxford or Cambridge, to Manchester or Liverpool or Birmingham and to a small sea-coast town on the Cornish coast.[1] Unfortunately the employers are not yet content, claiming at one time that *autonomous* District Trade Boards and not merely District Committees with advisory powers should be granted, at another that members of the National Federation of Merchant Tailors should be exempted from the operation of the Board, at another that exemption should apply to members of the Association of London Master Tailors or to all employing men exclusively on the one-man-one-job system (as it did under the original Trade Board established by the 1909 Act), at another, and most emphatically of all, that the Retail Tailoring Board should be dissolved altogether. With such feelings prevailing among the employers it is not surprising that a corresponding animosity has been displayed by the workers' representatives, and that as reported in the *Merchant Tailor* for March 1923, " the Retail Bespoke Tailoring Trade Board does not work well. A second reduction on 1st March, 1923 was only secured after a threat by the employers to resign."

While it is a little difficult to believe that the Retail Tailoring Board has had such universally disastrous effect on the trade as the employers would have us believe, there is no doubt that some rural districts have been badly hit. Insufficient notice was taken by Trade Union leaders, anxious to establish a progressively rising *National Minimum Standard* of wages on a uniform scale, of the special conditions which prevail in the villages. The sufferings of the rural tailor, as of the rural dressmaker, in recent years, must for the most part indeed be attributed to the inevitable march of events, on which stress

---

[1] It has been the practice of the Retail Tailoring Board almost invariably to adopt the recommendations of the District Committees in framing its own recommendations to the Minister of Labour.

has been laid both elsewhere in these pages, and by other observers. It is all the more important that these should not be aggravated by the ignorance of local conditions natural in a comparatively small body of men, nearly all drawn from the towns. The District Committees which have now been functioning for some years may help to counteract this danger.

It remains to consider the question of the efficiency with which the Trade Board regulations are administered and the extent to which they are evaded. That there is evasion, and in some cases serious evasion, is beyond dispute. Any Trade Union official will say as much, and many will bring chapter and verse in incontestable proof. The employers' organizations also admit it, and frequently, indeed, base their criticisms of the Boards on the claim that evasion of legal rates is easy, and that a premium is thus set on illegality. Accordingly we find that in 1924 the National Federation of Merchant Tailors, at its Annual Conference at Blackpool, passed a resolution " That in view of the fact that numbers of workers in the West of England are now defeating the regulations of the Trade Board by working for rates considerably below the minimum in order to get a living, we ask the Minister of Labour to investigate the conditions of the trade in those districts, with a view to protecting those employers and workers who are working under serious difficulties by complying with the Trade Board rates. . . ." The mover of this resolution, Mr A. S. Cotterell, complained of collusion between employers and workers in the south-western area. He quoted an instance where a man was only being paid £2 a week. He personally requested the Trade Board inspector to investigate the position, and the latter found the books were in order, and signed, to the effect that the man's pay was to be £3 a week. Similar expressions of opinion are constantly to be found in the writings and speeches of representative employers. There is no need to add further instances here, or to quote from Trade Union publications, or from the public and private utterances of Trade Union officials, who naturally hold the view that evasions are of frequent occurrence even more strongly than do the employers.

What weight of statistical evidence can be adduced in support of the opinions thus expressed ? The number of employees on behalf of whom arrears of wages were claimed by the Ministry of Labour in the years 1923 and 1924 are given in the following Table :

Trade	Number of Workers on behalf of whom Arrears were Claimed		Total Amount Claimed	
	1923	1924	1923	1924
Corset	11	8	£ 58	£ 56
Dressmaking (E. and W.) .	978	794	3113	2930
,, (Scotland) . .	50	89	290	285
Millinery (E. and W.) . .	573	308	2630	1810
,, (Scotland) . .	47	2	122	8
Shirt-making	157	224	187	589
Retail Bespoke Tailoring . .	117	376	1657	2668
Wholesale Tailoring . .	282	748	1021	1183
Mantles	54	54	240	156
Total . .	2799	2603	9318	9385

In view of the numbers of workers engaged in the clothing trades these totals appear at first sight to be reasonably small. Further examination, however, is required. About three-fifths of the claims were made as the result of investigations made after complaints had been received, and about two-fifths as the result of routine inspections where no previous complaints had been received. The total number of routine inspections was about twice as large as the total number of inspections made specially after a complaint had been lodged. It thus appears that the chance of a claim being made as a result of a routine inspection is about one-sixth of the chance that it will be made after an inspection resulting from a complaint. It is also probable that the cases of under-payment leading to complaints will be more serious than those discovered in routine inspections, though the detailed figures of amounts claimed do not lend any very emphatic support to this view. What is important is that the total number of inspections, routine or otherwise, is very small compared with the number of firms on the books of the office of Trade Boards, as will be seen from the following Table :

Trade	Number of Establishments on Trade Board Lists		Total Number of Inspections (Routine and on Complaint)		Number of Establishments from which Arrears were Claimed	
	1923	1924	1923	1924	1923	1924
Corset	502	468	17	49	8	8
Dressmaking (E. and W.)	10,871	11,657	552	457	196	179
,, (Scotland)	3,589	2,663	66	100	22	14
Millinery (E. and W.) .	14,798	12,574	663	353	187	119
,, (Scotland) .	3,144	2,155	57	57	19	2
Shirt-making . . .	1,315	1,347	47	85	9	27
Tailoring Retail Bespoke	18,628	20,002	309	630	103	179
Tailoring Wholesale .	4,700	4,884	225	322	79	111
Wholesale Mantle . .	2,123	2,405	86	115	19	30
Total . .	59,170	60,155	2022	2168	642	667

It will be seen that the number of firms from which arrears were claimed amounts to nearly a third of the number inspected, and that, on the other hand, the number of firms inspected in any one year was only about one-thirtieth of the total number registered. There must thus be vast numbers of firms which have never yet been inspected at all, especially when it is remembered that in many cases inspections are probably made of firms which have already been inspected once and found to be guilty of under-payment. It can therefore scarcely be doubted that the cases of evasion of Trade Board minimum rates are very numerous, and this view, as we have seen, is borne out by the opinions of many Trade Union officials as well as of a fair number of employers. Breaches of the Trade Boards Act other than under-payment have also been fairly frequent. These usually take the form either of failure to post notices of minimum rates or failure to keep adequate Wages Record. As they are most often associated with firms found to be guilty also of under-payment they are, however, of minor interest.

It is difficult to see how substantially better results can be achieved with the inspectorate at the Ministry's disposal. At the end of 1923, with a total of 180,000 firms in all Trade Board trades on the Ministry's list, the staff of inspectors amounted to 40, of whom 11 were loaned from other departments. In 1924, sanction was obtained for a permanent staff of 60. This means roughly one inspector for each 3000 firms, an obviously ludicrous proportion if rigid enforcement of the law is to be achieved. It is seldom possible for an inspector to visit more than one or two firms in a day, and inspections often occupy even longer than this. It appears that on the average about 100 inspections per head of the staff are made annually, so that to ensure one inspection per annum for each firm would involve an increase in the number of inspectors to 1800. On grounds of economy such a figure is quite out of the question, nor is it really necessary, as the fear of an inspection and prosecution, if the chances that it will occur were at all considerable, would be an adequate incentive to obey the law. Even as matters stand to-day, there can be no doubt that Trade Board legislation has been of very substantial value to the employees even of those firms guilty of occasional illegalities. Nor is it everybody who requires constant supervision to ensure that he will obey the law. It must be left to the judgment of the reader whether some increase in the staff of inspectors might not be justified, even in these times when every extra penny spent by Government departments is a source of anxiety for the Chancellor of the Exchequer.

CHAPTER V

THE WAGE LEVEL AND METHODS OF WAGE PAYMENT

THE most striking feature which the clothing industries present to the student of wages problems is the diversity in methods of remuneration which prevails.

A second very marked characteristic is (or was, for the Trade Boards Acts have gone far to promote uniformity in the wholesale sections of the industry) the wide range within which the earnings of individual workers may lie. In the past, with no authoritative wage-fixing bodies in existence outside the retail tailoring trades, employers paid whatever their workers could be got to accept, and this amount varied enormously from town to town, from process to process, and from firm to firm. In the case of retail tailoring properly agreed-on lists of " log "-rates have long been in use, but here, too, there was a very great diversity between different districts, while the predominant part played by seasonal fluctuations in employment made the actual logs almost useless as guides to the average yearly earnings of representative workers.

A third point which arrests attention is the considerable improvement which has taken place in the earnings of almost all classes of clothing workers, and especially of the less highly skilled grades, since pre-war days. We may briefly discuss this point before going on to consider the methods of remuneration and scales of earnings at present in vogue.

(a) THE RISE IN WAGES SINCE 1914

Before the war, earnings in all the wholesale sections of the clothing trades were admittedly low. Almost equally low, though this fact was less in evidence at the time, because high hourly rates obscured the fact of low annual earnings, were those in the retail sections. The most reliable guide in these matters is the Board of Trade Report on Earnings and Hours in 1906, from which we learn that the average remuneration in the firms dealt with, excluding outworkers, for the last week of September, 1906, was as follows : Men, 30s. 2d. ; Boys, 9s. 8d. ; Women, 13s. 6d. ; Girls, 5s. 9d. As has already been pointed out, these general results conceal wide differences in individual cases, and particularly between skilled and un-skilled, slow workers and fast workers, and London, provincial towns and country districts. For the south-west of England, especially, they give far too rosy a picture, while for towns like Leeds they err in the other direction. Somewhat fuller details regarding these points will be found in the final chapter of this book, in which a general comparison is drawn between present-day and pre-war conditions.

During the earlier years of the war, wages in the clothing trades, as in other industries, failed to keep pace with the rising cost of living, but in the latter half of the period of hostilities, and still more after the Armistice and the establish-ment of Trade Boards for all clothing workers, the lag was more than made good. The following detailed list of the advances in the tailoring trades, which is taken from the Ministry of Labour *Gazette*, can be roughly paralleled in other sections of the industry :

WAGES IN THE TAILORING TRADE (E. AND W.), 1914 TO 1921.

Section.	Hourly Wage in December of each Year.								Maximum Advance on pre-war.
	1914.	1915.	1916.	1917.	1918.	1919.	1920.	1921 (June).	
Journeymen Tailors. (London) .	(7½d.)[1]	(7½d.)[1]	(7½d.)[1]	(8d.)[1]	(10½d.)[1]	(1/1d.)[1]	(1/3d.)[1]	(1/1½d.)[1]	100%
Ready-made and Wholesale Bespoke	...	...	...	...	...	...	...	...	...
Measure Cutters. (London) . .	10d.[2]	10d.[2]	10d.[2]	11d.[2]+1½d.[4]	1/-+3d.[4]	1/-+3d.[4]	1/11¼d.[3]	2/2¼d.[3]	162%
Cutters and Knifemen. (London) .	10d.[2]	10d.[2]	10d.[2]	11d.[2]+1½d.[4]	1/-[2]+3d.[4]	1/-[2]+3d.[4]	1/9¼d.[3]	2/0¼d.[3]	142%
Measure Cutters. (Provinces) . .	9½d.[2]	9½d.[2]	9½d.[2]	9½d.[2]+1½d.[4]	9½d.[2]+3d.[4]	1/5d.[3]	1/9d.[3]	2/-[3]	153%
Knifemen and Pressers-off. (Provinces)	8¾d.[2]	8¾d.[2]	8¾d.[2]	8¾d.[2]+1½d.[4]	8¾d.[2]+3d.[4]	1/5d.[3]	1/7d.[3]	1/10d.[3]	151%
Stock Cutters and Fitters-up . .	8¼d.[2]	8¼d.[2]	8¼d.[2]	8¼d.[2]+1½d.[4]	8¼d.[2]+3d.[4]	1/5d.[3]	1/7d.[3]	1/10d.[3]	167%
Tailors and Passers	do.[2]	do.[2]	do.[2]	do.[2][4]	do.[2][4]	do.[3]	do.[3]	do.[3]	167%
Men (Unclassified), 22 years and over	6d.[3]	6d.[3]	6d.[3]	7d.-8d.[3]+1½d.[4]	8d.[3]+3d.[4]	1/1d.[3]	1/2d.[3]	1/4¼d.[3]	171%
Women, 18 years and over . .	3¼d.[3]	3½d.[3]	3½d.[3]	4d.-4½d.[3]+1d.[4]	5d.[3]+2d.[4]	8½d.[3]	9¼d.[3]	10d.	208%

Hours—48-50 (in 1914); 48 (in 1918).

[1] Rate per "log" hour (about 30 mins.' work).
[2] Trade Union Standard Rate per hour.
[3] Trade Board General Minimum Rate. Piece-workers are entitled to a minimum basis time-rate fixed at 1½d. per hour above the general minimum time-rate for men, and 1d. per hour above the general minimum time-rate for women.
[4] Award of Committee on Production.

It will be seen that the advance in the tailoring trades was greatest for women workers. In the rest of the clothing trades the workers are almost exclusively women, and it may safely be said that they benefited to at least an equal degree.

The following paragraph, dealing with wage-movements in the years immediately succeeding the war is based on the periodical reviews of wage changes to be found in the Ministry of Labour *Gazette*.

In the case of the workers engaged in the making of women's and children's clothing generally, minimum rates under the Trade Boards Act were first fixed in 1919. These rates were substantially increased in 1920. In 1921 the fall in prices had begun and the wage-rates either remained unchanged or began to fall. In the case of female workers in the Ready-made, Wholesale Bespoke and Retail Bespoke tailoring trades rates were reduced, and reductions for both male and female workers occurred in the Corset trade. In the case of females in the Wholesale Mantle and Costume trade, there were increases and decreases which left the minimum rates at the same level at the end as at the beginning of the year. No change occurred for adults in the Hat, Cap and Millinery, and the Shirt-making trades. In the Dressmaking and Women's Light Clothing trades certain classes of women received an increase, whilst other classes of adults received no change. In 1922 reductions took place all along the line, both in the rates fixed by the Trade Boards and in those arrived at by separate agreement between employers and Trade Unions. By the end of this year the fall showed signs of coming to an end, though further reductions, amounting to an average drop of 10 per cent., were made in 1923. In 1924 and subsequent years only minor adjustments were effected. A list of Trade Board Minimum Rates, as at 31st December 1924 and 31st December 1925 is subjoined :

TRADE BOARD MINIMUM RATES.

Trade Board.	Lowest Grade of Adult Female.		Lowest Grade of Adult Male (at 22 years of age).	
	31st Dec. 1924.	31st Dec. 1925.	31st Dec. 1924.	31st Dec. 1925.
Corset	7d.	7d.	1/1d.	1/1d.
Dressmaking and Women's Light Clothing (E. and W.) R.B. Section	6¾d., 7d., 7½d. (ac'ding to pop	6¾d., 7d., 7½d. ulation of town)	1/-	1/-
Others	7d.	7d.	1/-	1/-
Dressmaking. etc. (Scotland) R.B. Section	7d., 7½d. (ac'ding to pop	7d. 7½d. ulation of town)	1/2d.	1/2d.
Others	6⅓d.	6½d.	...	1/2d.
Hat, Cap and Millinery (E. and W.)	7d.	7d.	1/1d.	1/1d.
Hat, Cap, etc. (Scotland)	...	...	1/2d.	...
Wholesale Cloth, Hat and Cap Section	7½d.	7½d.	...	1/2d.
Others	7d., 7½d.	7d., 7½d.	...	1/2d.
Linen and Cotton Handkerchief	6½d.	6½d.	1/-	1/-
Made-up Textiles	6¼d.	6¼d.	10¾d.	10¾d.
Ostrich and Fancy Feather	7d.	7d.	1/-	1/-
Ready-made and Wholesale Bespoke Tailoring	6½d.	7d.	10¾d.	11¼d.
Retail Bespoke Tailoring (as fixed by original Board)	7½d.	7½d.	1/-	1/-
Shirt-making	6½d.	7d.	1/2d.	1/2d.
Wholesale Mantle and Costume	6½d.	7d.	10½d.	10½d.

Note.—The above minimum rates are on the average slightly higher than those fixed in other Trade Board trades.

(b) EXISTING METHODS OF REMUNERATION AND EARNINGS

In this section we shall outline the various methods by which wages are at the present day being calculated, and attempt a rough estimate of what the average worker actually earns.

There are three methods of remuneration in use in the clothing trades, namely (a) Time-rates ; (b) Straightforward Piece-rates ; (c) " Log "-rates, the latter being only used in the retail tailoring industry. The task of examining these will be simplified by treating the wholesale and retail trades separately.

In the wholesale or factory sections of the clothing industry, the general rule is that piece-rates are paid, time-rates being reserved for the small minority of cases where piece-rates are either impossible or obviously inequitable. The impossible cases include, on the one hand, supervisory work, such as that of the foreman and passers, and on the other hand, work which is constantly varied, such as that of a machinist engaged entirely in alteration-work. The cases where piece-rates would be inequitable are those where the worker must be constantly at his post, although the volume of work is fluctuating. This is generally true of the cutter's work, though cutters are often paid piece-wages ; as well as of some of the pressing. It is, of course, also true of the packing and warehouse staff. A special case is that of the learner who is at first paid a small time-rate, and is only put on a piece-rate when she has attained sufficient speed to earn more in that way. The time required for the attainment of this standard naturally varies considerably, ranging from a few weeks to several years, according to the intricacy of the work and the thoroughness of the training. Time-rates are also paid to those grades of workers which a firm is particularly anxious to keep on, even in times of depression, either because of the intrinsic skill required for their work, or because it is of a kind in which the worker improves with long experience in the same firm, adapting himself or herself to its particular requirements. This is perhaps the chief reason for paying time-rates to cutters. Each firm has its own particular clientele and its own particular styles, and these call for as much continuity of service as possible in the cutting-room.

The fixing of time-rates, at least of minimum time-rates, presents no difficulties to the individual employer, since these are prescribed for him by the appropriate Trade Board. In the case of piece-rates the Trade Board merely prescribes an hourly rate, which is always higher than the minimum time-rate, as the basis on which piece-rates must be fixed for the normal worker, and the actual fixing of the rates has to be done by the foreman, with or without a consultation with the workers. Frequently cases are found of agreements between a Trade Union branch and the local employers for the payment of a rate in excess of the minimum, provision being sometimes also made for an annual holiday on full pay. These agreements are specially common in the case of cutters who, in the factories, are usually more highly organized than the other workers. In the London area the London Employers' Association has entered into such agreements with the unions concerned, in all the branches of the industry in which its members are engaged ; and these agreements cover all grades both on time and piece, including learners. In Wigan, West Ham and Bethnal Green the Town Councils insert a " fair wages " (i.e. the rates fixed by collective agreement or in practice paid by good employers) clause into their clothing contracts.

A correct estimate of actual wages earned by the different grades is particularly difficult, owing to the immense amount of short-time worked in slack periods. This varies with different sections of the trade, and with individual firms.

H

Some managements succeed in keeping their hands at work almost all the year round, by one device or another. Sometimes stock articles are made in the slack time. Sometimes the employees inside the factory are kept fully employed at the expense of home-workers, whose services are only enlisted in the busy season. In other firms most grades of employees are liable to periodical dismissal and re-engagement, while nearly all are compelled to resort now and then to short-time. Broadly speaking, the wholesale bespoke trade is more seasonal than the ordinary wholesale trade ; while outer clothing and mantles are more seasonal than underclothing, light dressmaking and shirts. In a fairly good year the regular employees of a well-organized factory do not get a very excessive amount of short-time, and even this, as far as wages are concerned, is perhaps made up for by the extra overtime earnings in the busy season. But recently very few years have been "fairly good."

A further circumstance which makes detailed lists of piece-rates uninformative, is the fact that tasks which are closely similar in appearance often vary considerably in the ease or difficulty with which they may be performed. For these reasons, and to avoid unduly weighting the text with statistical matter, such lists have been relegated to Appendix V.

Even average weekly earnings are hard to gauge, owing to the very wide spread between those of an exceptionally fast worker and an ordinary worker on the one hand, and an ordinary and a slow worker on the other. Then again, a great deal depends on the degree of organizing capacity displayed by the person in charge of the particular worker's room. Two men of about equal capacity, and employed on the same work at the same rates, but under different foremen, may find that their wages differ at the end of the week by a large percentage.

On the basis, however, of a 48-hour week of full employment, a fair estimate of average earnings would be the following :

		Per week.
Cutters		75s.
Male Tailors		75s.
Tailoresses		45s.
Machinists, etc.		30s. to 35s.

Earnings in a full week of less than 30s. on the part of all but a few specially slow adult workers are undoubtedly rare. There are variations between one district and another ; isolated country factories being at the bottom, and some of the high-grade Leeds firms at the top of the scale. The wholesale clothing trade generally pays slightly higher rates than the shirt and dressmaking (factory) trades. In the majority of cases Trade Board rates [1] are observed, neither more nor less being paid, and where this is so, the minimum weekly earnings, on the basis of a full week's work, can easily be ascertained by consulting the rates as they are periodically fixed.

The Trade Board regulations, as well as the agreements between bodies of employers and workers, usually provide for the payment of overtime wages for all hours worked over those which have been laid down as "normal." These may be taken to be 9 hours per day on ordinary days and 5 on Saturdays, with a weekly maximum of 48. In cases where a 5-day week is worked, 9½ hours is regarded as the "normal day." For hours worked in excess of these, payment must be made at the rate of time-and-a-quarter for the first two hours in excess, and time-and-a-half thereafter, as well as for all excess hours on Saturdays.[2] Work performed on Sundays[2] or public holidays must be paid for at double rates. It may be noted that this provision, while it does not in so many words impose a legal maximum working-day, has the effect of securing

[1] Published in *Ministry of Labour Gazette*.
[2] For Jewish workers Saturdays and Sundays change places.

that the normal hours worked do not exceed 48 per week. In practice they now vary for a worker not on short-time from 44 to 48, perhaps the commonest figure being 47. This is in accordance with post-war practice in other similar industries and represents a substantial reduction from the 56-hour weeks and 60-hour weeks, and even some improvement on the 50-hour Trade Union week, which prevailed in 1913. It is indeed not the least of the benefits which the workers in the clothing industries owe to the Trade Boards and to the humanitarian sentiment which prompted their establishment, that hours have been shortened.

The foregoing wages have, of course, been quoted for workers employed inside the factories or workshops. In the case of outworkers, weekly earnings are quite impossible to estimate, owing to the varied conditions under which work is done. Many outworkers only devote their spare time to sewing, others are employed very intermittently, while yet others are, in some way or other, unable to work at normal speed. All that can be said is that payment is on about the same piecework basis as that for women-workers inside the factories.

When we come to the retail trade, whether handicraft or subdivisional, the lack of uniformity is bewildering. We will first consider the handicraft section, where the method of payment known as the " log " prevails. This is really a schedule of piece-rates masquerading under the guise of time-rates. There are several such logs in operation in different parts of the country, the London log being by far the most important. Not only are there more handicraft tailors in London than in any other centre, but there is an increasing tendency for the London log to supersede those previously in operation elsewhere ; at the present time about 40 per cent. of the members of the A.S.T. & T. throughout the country work to it. It is, however, contended by the employers that the London log is not adapted in its present form to

national requirements.[1] Manchester, for instance, which until
1923 worked to the London log, is now party to a special
" Lancashire log," which is in operation throughout East
Lancashire and Westmoreland. Some of the provincial logs
are most unsatisfactory in their actual results, so that in some
cases a tailor will get paid for a garment in which there has
been a substantial amount of machining, more than for one
which he has made throughout by hand. Of the London
log, the chief complaint that can perhaps be made is that
it is needlessly cumbersome, and that it would be much
simpler to abandon it in favour of straight piece-rates. It has,
however, the sanction of immemorial usage, and by repeated
modification has been brought to a high state of perfection.
As it now stands, it represents an agreement arrived at between
the Association of London Master Tailors on the one hand, and
the London branches of the Amalgamated Society of Tailors
and Tailoresses and the Tailors' and Garment Workers' Trade
Union on the other, as to the amount of time which shall be
allowed for the purpose of wage calculations, for each operation
in the making of the various garments. Periodical adjustments
are arranged in order to make allowance for changes in styles
which affect the amount of workmanship required for the
different parts of a garment. There are separate logs for

---

[1] At a meeting of the London Area Committee of the National
Federation of Merchant Tailors in 1922, " it was regretted that the
appointed members of the Trade Board seemed to regard the London
' log ' as a national ' log,' as it was not at all suited for general adoption
in its present form. It was the insistence of the Piece-rates Sub-Com-
mittee on using this ' log ' as the basis, in which they were supported
by the Board, that resulted in the employers' representative refusing to
continue to serve on that Committee. . . . The London ' log ' required
considerable revision before it would be at all suitable for adoption as a
national ' log,' it having been compiled in accordance with West End
requirements and not from a provincial standpoint." The real objection underlying this complaint appears to be that the London " log "
gives very generous time-allowances for the various processes, and thus
involves the payment of comparatively low hourly " log "-rates. This,
the employers feel, creates a false impression in the minds of the workers
that they are being underpaid. (*Vide infra.*)

Court dresses, for military tailoring, and so on. The unit of work adopted is the " log " hour. Each part of the garment is reckoned to require so many " log " hours and minutes for the making. By adding these together the total " log " time for the garment is arrived at. Where machining is done, there is a proportionate reduction in the " log " time allowed. Payment is then made at a " log time-rate," which is periodically fixed by agreement. There is no pretence that the " log " hour is equivalent to a real hour. Actually it is probably nearer 35 or 40 minutes. All that matters, it is argued, is that the time allotted to each operation shall be in correct proportion to those allotted to the others. Provided this is so, rates will be fairly adjusted between one worker and another, and it makes no difference whether a worker is paid, say, 7d. for a log hour of 35 minutes or 1s. for a real time hour. The log hour is one of those fictions dear to the British heart. In point of fact, however, the discrepancy between the log hour and the hour according to the Astronomer Royal, is not entirely a matter of no consequence. In negotiations about wages it is freely admitted that the discrepancy exists, but its extent affords constant matter for dispute. Furthermore, though the instructed Trade Union official may know better, the ordinary working tailor is apt to compare his wage-rates unfavourably with those of workers in other occupations where wages are simply paid by time ; and when the difference between the two systems is pointed out to him, he may none the less claim that a " log " hour is a " real hour's work," and that the fact that he always accomplishes it in 35 minutes is merely a proof of his own superior capacity as compared with less gifted and industrious mortals. And then, with more reason, the worker complains that employers are constantly trying to secure reductions of wages under the guise of increased time-reductions for machine-work.

This is only one criticism of the system. At least to a layman, the "log" seems full of unnecessary complexities. Perhaps this is not so, but there is undoubtedly a desire on the part of employers to substitute for it a simpler system of piece-rates, such as those in general use in the subdivisional systems.[1]

In some country districts the plan is adopted of paying straight piece-rates at so much a garment. Thus, in one country centre in 1922, the following scale prevailed :

Lounge coats . . .	17s.
Vests	5s. 6d.
Trousers	6s. 6d.

While this has the merit of simplicity, it is unsuitable where a large number of minor variations are required in the making of garments to suit the order of the individual customer ; and still more so where there is a wide range in the quality of the workmanship, and the proportion of machining to hand-work. It has been suggested in some quarters that a modification of the above system should replace payment by "log." For this purpose several styles of garment would be recognized, as, for instance, in the case of lounge coats, the following :

	Grade.
"Bagged" throughout	I
Inside collar, sleeves, pockets, tacked by hand . .	II
Same as II, with collar wholly made and put on by hand, linings felled in	III
Complete "open" coat	IV
Same as IV, but no machine work	V

A scale of this kind could be used for calculating both the journeyman's wages, and the price to be paid by a retailer to a subcontractor.

In other cases, such as those of the few handicraft tailors employed in factories, or of the employees of firms which are

---

[1] A detailed example of Log-rates will be found in Appendix IIIA.

parties to the London Employers' Association, payment is made simply by time, or " clock-hour." Time-rates have this advantage over " log "-rates for handicraft tailoring, that they offer no inducement to the tailor to scamp his work. In the past the spirit of craftsmanship has perhaps proved an adequate safeguard against this, but whether it will continue to do so in the face of the present shortage of labour and decay of long-term apprenticeship remains to be seen. Perhaps the log system is merely one symptom of the spirit of craftsmanship itself—for there was never a body of highly-skilled workers, in any field, which did not dearly love a mystery or two in connection with its trade—to be a symbol of its own exclusiveness and superiority over the common herd. However this may be, the London log is at the moment being adopted throughout the country, and the Trade Board has actually fixed " log "-rates. (This was done in spite of the protests of the *employers* representatives, who claim that the London log is not adapted to the methods of work prevalent in other centres, and who absented themselves from all the meetings at which the subject was brought up for discussion.) Thus it would seem that, far from disappearing, the " log "-system is likely to be more firmly entrenched in the future than it has been in the past.

In the subdivisional trade, piece-wages and time-wages seem to be paid almost indiscriminately, the latter being, perhaps, the more commonly found. The small master is himself paid so much a garment for the making, and his problem is to devise methods of work and remuneration which will leave the margin between the amount he receives and the amount he pays to his workpeople as large as possible. Usually the easiest way to do this is by time-wages, combined with a strict system of surveillance and a constant application of pressure to the work-people to speed up output. If a piece-rate is paid, it is true that the worker will probably exert himself to the utmost, but most small masters reckon to secure this desirable result without incurring the sacrifice of profits involved in the payment of a piece-rate! The payment of piece-rates is further apt to invite comparisons between the master's income and outlay, which will not be favourable to his reputation for generosity, and which may quite possibly ignore some vital consideration in his favour. Where the rates are calculated on an elaborate system, and especially where the number of different workers in a team is large, this is a point of minor importance, as it will be hard for the employees to work out exactly how much the master has to pay in wages for each garment. On the other hand, if the number of different workers on the garment is small, and payment is made to each in a round sum for the whole of the work he has done on each garment, such calculations can be made with fatal ease. The chief incentive to pay piece-rates from the master's point of view is the desire to keep the workers up to the scratch in the matter of output; in small shops where the master is himself always on the spot, and works in company with his employees, he can achieve this end by other means, and the incentive is lacking. In large subdivisional shops, however, piece-wages are usually paid.

Whichever method is adopted, earnings in the subdivisional trades tend to be high. While the factory-owners are always eager to get special permits of exemption from Trade Board rates for their slow workers, the typical Jewish subcontractor prefers not to bother about this, but to avoid slow workers like the plague. It is claimed by the officials of the Master Tailors' Association that subcontractors in the West End never pay women-workers less than 10d. per hour, and that men tailors earn at least 14s. per day and often as much as £1 or £1, 5s. On the basis of a 48-hour week these minimum rates would work out at 40s. a week for women and 75s. for men, *i.e.* about 25 per cent. above Trade Board rates. No doubt exceptions can be found, and other centres might reach a slightly lower standard, but these figures may safely be regarded as normal for a large proportion of the workers. At the same time it must be remembered that the subdivisional trade is considerably more subject to seasonal fluctuations than the factory trade, so that the discrepancy in annual earnings is less than might appear at first sight. A typical set of wages for a team in the West End would be as follows :

	£	s	d
Machinists (women), each	£3	0	0
Tailors (men), each	5	0	0
Pressers (men), each	4	0	0
Work-hands (women), each	2	10	0

In addition, the team might include learners at very much lower wages.

(c) DEDUCTIONS FROM WAGES

There remains to be considered the question of deductions from wages. These fall into four classes, namely : (a) fines for unpunctuality, breaches of workshop and factory regulations, etc. ; (b) excessive charges for sewing materials, etc., where these are paid for by the worker, and for damages for which the worker is responsible ; (c) non-payment for " waiting-time " ; and (d) the " dead-horse " system.

The first of these deductions is definitely illegal. At one time it was a favourite means of reducing real wages. The lengths to which it was pushed are familiar to readers of Mr and Mrs Hammond's *Town Labourer*, where we find quoted a list of the fines to which a spinner at Tyldesley was subject in the year 1823.[1] While the state of affairs thus revealed has long disappeared, the practice of fining workers for breaches of discipline and for slight unpunctuality was still common

[1] J. L. and B. Hammond, *Town Labourer*, pp. 19-20.

thirty years ago.   At the present time it is virtually unknown.

The second type of deduction, on the other hand, is fairly common. In cases where expensive materials have to be used, there can of course be no objection to charging work-people for the quantity they use as a precaution against waste or dishonesty, provided this is a recognized practice, and due allowance is made for it in fixing the wage-rate ; but frequently the prices charged are greater than the materials' real value. In other cases where a large variety of costly silks are required for embroidery, no allowance is made for " sewings " which the worker has paid for but not used ; this occurs in the millinery and dressmaking trades, and may be a serious hardship. Yet another practice may occur, namely that of making work-people find their own sewings when they are only paid the bare Trade Board rates. This is, of course, quite illegal, and is now rare, even in connection with outwork.

Non-payment for " waiting-time " is probably the commonest abuse to be found in connection with wage payment. As the law very properly stands, a worker kept with the employer's knowledge and consent, expressed or implied, on the employer's premises, in˙ the hope of being given work, must be paid at the minimum time-rate throughout the period of waiting. This time is very frequently *not* paid for at all. Not only is this the case with outworkers who may arrive early in the morning and be kept hanging about for several hours, before either being given work or told definitely that none is to be had for the day ; it is also not unusual for the work-people in the factory after doing, say, a couple of hours' work, to be told there is nothing more for them for the time being, but that, if they will " clock out " and wait about, more may turn up later, in which case they " clock in " again when it comes, thus only getting paid for the time during which they are actually at work. This is a very difficult practice to check, as the workers are strongly tempted to connive at it in the fear that otherwise they will lose the chance of getting any work that may be available.

The " dead-horse " system is of very old standing. It arose out of the practice on the part of employers of lending money to their work-people in hard times for purchases of food and other necessities, the money so lent being repaid in kind, that is in labour, at a later date. Under this system, workers sometimes became so heavily indebted to their masters as to be virtually their slaves. While this practice is highly objectionable, there is nothing in the least illegal about it. Since the coming of Trade Boards, however, it has been made the occasion for the evasion of Trade Board rates. Piece-workers who fail, owing to the insufficient provision of work, or because the piece-rates are really fixed too low, to earn the minimum time-rates, are paid these rates and credited in the wage statements with the full work necessary to earn them. A note is kept of the difference between the work they actually have done, and the work for which they have been paid, and in busy times this extra work has to be done gratuitously, before any extra payment is allowed. This is quite illegal, and though not very common, still prevails in some places, especially in London.

In all these ways the net wages are here and there reduced. Such reductions amount, however, to a minute proportion of the total wages bill. It is safe to assume that if the *nominal* weekly wage of a clothing worker is known, so also is the amount which will find its way into his or her pocket on Friday night.

CHAPTER VI

TRADE UNIONS

THE history of trade unionism in the clothing industries is an epitome of the struggle between rival principles of workers' organization which has been waged in the national field for over a century. The two leading unions are the Amalgamated Society of Tailors and Tailoresses—conservative, pacific, and organized on craft lines; and the Tailors' and Garment Workers' Trade Union (formerly the United Garment Workers' Union)—radical, active, and adhering to the philosophy of industrial unionism. In addition to these bodies there are a few small organizations mainly covering single districts or single crafts, and frequently confined to members of a particular race or sex. Especially common is it to find a group of perhaps a few hundred or even a few score Jewish workers in a particular town with an organization of their own. At one time or another such bodies have appeared in Leeds, Birmingham, Manchester, London,[1] and elsewhere. Sometimes they have enjoyed a relatively long life, more often they have sprung into existence as the result of a temporary grievance, only to die away or to be incorporated in the ranks of a larger body after a few months or years of hectic and precarious life. A more numerous section of the organized workers in the clothing trades is to be found in the ranks of various general labour unions—especially the Shop Assistants' Union and the National Union of General Workers. In London, for instance, the needlewomen and milliners employed in the workshops of

[1] There is, for instance, at the present time a small society in East London known as the Jewish Ladies' Tailors' Society.

large department stores are nearly all thus organized. Some of the employees in the East End factories in these trades have also been enrolled, in spite of the objections raised by the Tailors' and Garment Workers' Trade Union. During the war the general unions secured many thousands of such workers. A great number have since left the ranks of trade unionism altogether; others have been captured by the Garment Workers' organization, which has also absorbed most of the sectional unions previously alluded to, and is in fact rather the result of a series of amalgamations and absorptions, than a body which has grown as a separate entity from small dimensions to its present considerable scale.

With such diversity of aim and method, it is not surprising that there has been continual strife, sometimes open, sometimes subterranean. The details of this strife, which reveal a sordid history of cut-throat competition for members in industrial towns, of scurrilous attacks on rival leaders, and of failure to unite in the common interest in moments of emergency are of little importance. The clash of principles ever present in the background, on the other hand, is of considerable significance to the social philosopher.

The Amalgamated Society of Tailors and Tailoresses dates back some sixty years to the days following the " New Model " of 1851, when the first of the great modern craft unions, the Amalgamated Society of Engineers, was founded on the ruins of the militant unionism of Owenite days. In the 50's and the 60's the lead given by the Engineers was followed by many bodies of skilled workers, among others by the handicraft tailors, who formed an amalgamation of several small societies in 1866, starting with a membership of about 2000. The union thus founded has survived intact to the present day, though with the decay of the handicraft tailor much of its old prestige has gone. Its members during the war rose at one time to some 40,000; to-day it can only boast of perhaps 13,000, many of whom are women. In the early days of its existence, and indeed until the war period, the A.S.T. & T. confined its efforts to organizing the skilled handicraft tailors. Except in Scotland, where a separate society gradually won over its members, it was almost the only union in this trade until 1905, when a split, to be described later on, occurred in the ranks of the West End operatives, a portion of them forming an independent union which later decided to give its adherence to the United Garment Workers' Trade Union, a body which had hitherto confined itself to the wholesale trade. Although the Amalgamated Society of Tailors and Tailoresses was originally formed in Manchester, and its headquarters are still located in that city, the West End is, of course, the principal seat of handicraft tailoring in the country, and the defection of several thousand members from the A.S.T. & T.'s West End branch was a severe blow. The subsequent entrance on the scene of the United Garment Workers' Trade Union meant inevitable trouble between the two bodies. The A.S.T. & T. officials regarded the action of the U.G.W.T.U. in admitting skilled handicraftsmen as a gross act of trespass. When the war broke out, bringing in its train an enormous accession of workers to the trade union movement, the A.S.T. & T. naturally felt justified in repaying the U.G.W.T.U. in kind by organizing branches of its own among factory workers throughout the country. The task was rendered easier by the fact that already in many factories men were to be found who had started out in life as tailors on the bench, and who on entering the factory, often as passers, had not discontinued their A.S.T. & T. membership. These individuals were able to organize their fellow-workers as members of the A.S.T. & T. An indiscriminate struggle for members thereupon began through anxiety to obtain new members in advance of its rival, each union failing to see that its own true interest would probably best be served by confining itself to its traditional field. Not stopping at this policy, the organizers of each of the two bodies in many cases made attempts to win over unionists who already belonged to the other organization, in the vain hope, perhaps, of ultimately exterminating it altogether. In the course of this struggle the A.S.T. & T. secured a permanent foothold among factory workers in a few provincial towns—notably Kettering, Plymouth and Huddersfield.[1] These branches which at one time boasted about 10,000 members between them, still account for about 2000. The London West End branch, which is so powerful as to be almost independent of headquarters, numbers another 600. Originally the London branch was a separate society, and only joined the A.S.T. & T. after its power had spread in the provinces. This circumstance naturally increased its sense of independence. The remaining 9000 members are organized in little branches throughout the country, including Ireland, where there are some 1200 members.[2] In Scotland there are only four such branches—at Dundee, Forfar, Aberdeen and Glasgow. At one time the union was as powerful in Scotland, especially outside Glasgow and Edinburgh, as in England, but gradually lost members to the Scottish Tailors' Union, which was led by an enthusiastic Secretary of the name of Craig. This body was about 4000 strong when it decided to throw in its lot with the 100,000 members of the United Garment Workers' Trade Union, in the hope that its position would thus be strengthened. The effects of this decision on the welfare of handicraft tailors in Scotland are open to dispute— anyhow the decision was a severe blow to Craig, who died shortly afterwards of disillusionment and frustrated hopes.

---

[1] In such cases, however, the A.S.T. & T. organizes the factory workers in a separate branch from that containing the handicraftsmen. This is not the method which an industrial union would naturally adopt.

[2] Out of a former total of 10,000. (*Vide infra.*)

The aims and methods of the A.S.T. & T. are those of the old-fashioned craft union. The objects as stated in the rules are " to maintain *as far as possible* [1] a uniform rate of wages for piece-work and a standard rate for day-work ; to protect its members from illegal or unjust stoppages, or unjust treatment of whatever nature employers may endeavour to subject them to. *To render assistance to its members in sickness and burial;* [1] and to regulate the relations between work-people and employers *by means of friendly representation and arbitration.*" [1] The strike weapon is specifically excluded, though on very rare occasions it has been employed. It was, indeed, a controversy over the desirability of employing this method of supporting the workers' interests that embittered the relations between the London branch and the rival organization which has now joined the U.G.W.T.U. At such times as the executive committee does authorize a strike, the conflict is usually confined to a single locality. Strike pay may then be issued by the branch concerned. In the section of the rules providing for this contingency the following additional note of warning to impetuous local officials is to be found : " It must be distinctly understood that all branches labouring under any grievance will use all legitimate means in their power to bring the matter to an amicable adjustment before requesting the aid of the Executive Council. In the event of such means failing, it will be the duty of the secretary in any town where a grievance exists to forward, in clear and lucid terms, the matter in dispute to the Executive Council, who shall take immediate steps to consider the case, and recommend a course of action. Any member, members or branch refusing to admit their dispute to arbitration for settlement shall not be entitled to any support from the society. . . . No branch shall use their branch funds for strike or lock-out purposes without first getting information that the Executive Council consider it a

---

[1] Italics mine.

I

bona fide case for support." [1]   The greater part of the funds are expended on friendly benefits, the management expenses being comparatively modest in dimension.   The majority of the branches are small enough for most of the work of organization to be done by honorary officials.   The branch treasurer receives 10s. per annum per 100 members ; the president is unpaid, except when the branch numbers over 200, in which case he is rewarded at the same rate as the treasurer.   The shop-stewards, whose duties are to collect contributions, receive a 5 per cent. commission for men, and 10 per cent. for women.[2] Only small expenses are incurred for rent, since it is usual to use a local public house as a club-house and the publican is usually willing to accept a very low payment for the use of his premises.   Only where a large number of women are members of the branch is the practice of the T. & G.W.T.U. of having a separate local office followed.

Between the local branch and headquarters there is no costly administrative system, nor are there special district organizers or other officials whose duties are mainly to conduct propaganda and enrol new members.   Indeed, in the case of a society whose scope lies primarily in so limited a field as that

---

[1] In the early days the strike was a little more popular with the A.S.T. & T. All through the 70's, 80's, and 90's, its policy was to single out a special town and organize a strike there, concentrating all its resources in money and leadership on the one locality. In this way small increases of pay were generally secured and conditions throughout the country improved gradually in a piecemeal fashion. (It must not be forgotten that at that time wage-rates were at the low level of about 2d. per log-hour.) In the 90's the National Federation of Merchant Tailors was founded, chiefly to counter this very policy by similar co-operation on the part of the employers, and in consequence, after one or two failures, the A.S.T. & T. almost abandoned the strike-weapon. In recent years the Society has only been concerned in three strikes of any magnitude ; in Dublin against outwork in 1900, in London for an increase of wages in 1912, and again in London against a decrease in 1921. Only the first of these was supported by headquarters ; it ended disastrously, there being more outwork after its conclusion than there had been to start with. The other two strikes we shall shortly discuss at greater length.

[2] These percentages apply also to the stewards of the T. & G.W.T.U.

of handicraft tailoring there would hardly be room for such officers. Each branch pays out friendly benefits from the moneys it collects, merely forwarding part of its balance at the end of the year to be paid into a Permanent Fund under the management of the Executive Committee. The headquarters staff is small and costs comparatively little to maintain, staff salaries amounting to less than £1000 out of a total expenditure of some £22,000. The only important paid officials are the Secretary and the Assistant-secretary (the latter having been for many years the wife of the former). The amount of routine work is so small that these two are quite able to cope with it without the appearance of being unduly pressed. Their activities are subject to the control of the Executive Committee, which meets at frequent intervals to decide questions of policy. More general questions and alterations in the rules are dealt with by a General Conference of delegates from the branches, which meets once every four years. This structure of branches with their officials, the small head office, executive committee, and general conference is in accordance with the time-honoured trade union forms, and is primitive in its simplicity when compared with the elaborate organizations which have been developed by some modern unions, such as for instance the Amalgamated Engineering Union.

The Tailors' and Garment Workers' Trade Union presents in its aims and methods a complete contrast with the Amalgamated Society of Tailors and Tailoresses. Its object is to organize in one body every one employed in the industry, in whatsoever capacity, and to improve the position of its members by a militant industrial and political campaign. Its very basis thus brings it into inevitable conflict with its elder brother.

The history of the union begins in Leeds, where a small society of operatives in the clothing factories was formed in 1889. At about the same time one or two other local unions of clothing workers came into existence in various parts of the country. One was situated in London, another in Bristol, while in Leeds itself the cutters in the wholesale clothing factories formed a separate little organization of their own. These bodies were merged with the original Leeds society to form a national union under the title of the Amalgamated Union of Clothing Operatives in the year 1894. This body started with a membership of about 500, which had risen to 1400 by the end of the century, at which level it remained for the next five years. By 1907 the numbers reached 2500, of whom 600 were women, and a rapid expansion from 1909 onwards brought them by 1915 up to 4000 men and 8000 women.

At this stage an amalgamation with several smaller unions took place, the numbers rising in consequence to 8000 men and 13,000 women, and the name of the society being changed into " The United Garment Workers' Trade Union." The bodies thus absorbed were " The Amalgamated Jewish Tailors, Machinists and Pressers," " The London and Provincial Cutters," " The London Jewish Tailors," " The Waterproof Garment Workers " (this union afterwards seceded and is now once more an independent body with about 1500 members and with Manchester as its headquarters), and " The London Society of Tailors and Tailoresses." This last body had broken away from the West End branch of the A.S.T. & T. in earlier years and now became the West End branch of the U.G.W.T.U., under circumstances which will hereafter be related in greater detail. During the war the United Garment Workers shared in the prosperity which was common to almost all trade unions throughout the industrial field. The peak was reached in July 1919 when the membership stood at 23,000 men and 79,000 women (after the accession of the " National Amalgamated Shirt, Collar and Jacket Society " had brought in an additional 6000 members).

By the end of 1920 the numbers had fallen to 87,000, in spite of the fact that further amalgamations took place in that year, the Belfast Shirt and Collar Society coming in with 2000 members, the Scottish Operative Tailors' and Tailoresses' Society (the counterpart in Scotland of the A.S.T. & T.) with 8000, and the Clothing Workers' Union with about 1500. In this year the title was again changed to its present form of "Tailors' and Garment Workers' Trade Union." In 1923 a low figure of 45,000 was reached. Naturally the decline in membership was greatest among the female workers. While in the four years from 1919 the number of men had only dropped from 23,000 to 14,000, of the 79,000 women of the peak year only 31,000 now remained. Most of the women had only been enrolled during the war-period of tumultuous unionism when work was plentiful, wages high, and subscriptions easily paid. When the slump came, many fell out of work, and many others dropped off from membership of a union which seemed unable, for the time being, to bring them any material reward. Since 1923 there has been a slight increase in the membership, which now stands at a figure of about 50,000.

It will be seen from the foregoing that compared with the slow and steady development of the A.S.T. & T., the growth of the Garment Workers' Union has been rapid. The absorption of all kindred unions, except the well-entrenched A.S.T. & T., accompanied by gains even at the latter's expense, affords a key to the general policy of enrolling "all grades" which has been pursued by the officials of the Union.

The chief strongholds of the union are Leeds with 7000 members, London with about 5000, Manchester with over 4000, Londonderry and Glasgow with 3000 each, Bristol with about 2000, Wigan and Hebden Bridge with rather fewer, and Edinburgh with about 1000. Some of these figures can be subjected to further analysis. In Leeds about two-thirds of

the members are factory workers and one-third subdivisional
tailors and tailoresses. In London the West End branch
accounts for perhaps 500 handicraft tailors, while the subdivisional membership amounts to about 2000. The bulk of
the remainder are in the wholesale tailoring trade, including
over 1000 cutters, but there are a few scattered workers in the
mantle, raincoat, artificial flower and other minor trades.
In Manchester the union includes very few of the subdivisional workers, but there are some 1600 shirt hands. The
remainder are practically all in the wholesale clothing trade.
In Derry shirts and collars rule the roost, and in Bristol,
Hebden Bridge and Wigan wholesale clothing. In Glasgow
the factory branch numbers about 1100 and the handicraft
tailoring branch about the same, while there are 600 subdivisional workers in the Union. In Edinburgh all the members
are handicraft tailors. Throughout Scotland, indeed, the
T. & G.W.T.U. has, with few exceptions, an almost 100 per
cent. membership among the handicraft tailors, whose decision
to throw in their lot with the English Union in 1920 has been
recorded above. It will be noticed that practically no workers
in the women's clothing trades have been enrolled.[1] In some
towns, notably London, many of these have joined the Shop
Assistants or General Workers.

When we examine the rules of the T. & G.W.T.U. we find
at once a striking contrast with those of the A.S.T. & T. The
objects are declared to be as follows :

" To regulate the number of apprentices ; to maintain a
fair standard wage, regular and uniform hours of labour and
honourable working conditions ; to provide for members who
may become unemployed, for the support of members in case
of sickness and accident, for the burial of members and their
wives ; to grant assistance in exceptional cases by means of a

[1] See Table on p. 135.

Benevolent Fund ; to render legal assistance ; to provide for superannuation . . . *to collect and maintain a Political Fund for the furtherance of the political objects mentioned in the Trade Union Act,* 1913 ; *to provide for the adoption of a Trade Union Label ; to promote the education of its members through a fund hereafter to be established, such education to be based on independent working-class principles ;* [2] to regulate the relations

[1] In this connection the following analysis of the membership in 1922 (according to the Trade Union Congress return) is of interest :

MEMBERSHIP OF TAILORS' AND GARMENT WORKERS' UNION

(For Trade Board Representation)

Section of Industry	Membership		
	Male	Female	Total
Ready-made and Wholesale Bespoke Tailoring	9,009	19,553	28,562
Subdivisional Workers	3,000	2,984	5,984
Retail Bespoke Tailoring	5,455	3,695	9,150
Wholesale Mantle and Costume . . .	500	1,659	2,159
Shirt and Collar	1,160	6,000	7,160
Hat and Cap (England and Wales) . .	300	1,000	1,300
,, ,, (Scotland)	20	60	80
Corset	20	328	348
Dressmaking and Women's Light Clothing (England)	50	750	800
Dressmaking and Women's Light Clothing (Scotland)	10	145	155
Ostrich and Fancy Feather and Artificial Flower . . . . . . Made-up Textiles . . . . . Cerement Making . . . . . Other Workers	88	600	688
	19,612	36,774	56,386

[2] Italics mine.

between employer and employed, and otherwise to further the interests of its members."

It will be seen that " political action " and " education on independent working-class principles " are among the objects above enumerated. The A.S.T. & T. makes no provision for either of these purposes. A large proportion of its members belongs, in fact, to either the Conservative or the Liberal Party, and the mere sound of the words "independent working-class principles " would send a shiver down the spines of its officials. The T. & G.W.T.U., on the other hand, is quite definitely left-wing in its political tendency, and several of its leading officials are well-known members of the Communistic " Minority Movement."

With such an outlook, it is not surprising that the Union looks with favour on a strike policy, as much because it helps to maintain the " class-struggle " as for any material benefits which it may confer. This inevitably means that a large proportion of the expenditure will be devoted to propaganda and organization, and that friendly benefits will take a back place. In several of the more important centres, notably Manchester, Bristol, London (East and West End branches), Glasgow, as well as the headquarters in Leeds, expensive offices and full-time secretaries are maintained. Between the head office and the branch officials stretches a hierarchy of permanent and temporary district organizers. The headquarters staff, besides the general secretary, treasurer. and assistant-secretary, includes a " general male organizer " and a " general woman organizer," while a considerable clerical staff is employed. As the administration of friendly benefits lies in the hands of the branches, this staff is principally employed in the work of organization and propaganda.

As in the case of the A.S.T. & T., general questions of policy are settled by the Executive Committee, which allows itself to be very largely guided by the headquarters permanent staff.

Supreme control lies in the hands of the General Conference, a body similar in structure and function to its namesake in the other union, but meeting every three instead of every four years.

It is not surprising to find that the differences already noted between the two societies extend to the personalities of their officials. The leaders of the A.S.T. & T. are thoroughly Conservative in outlook and temperament. Slow to take action, cautious perhaps to an excess, they confine themselves to upholding the sectional interest of their members and to endeavouring to maintain the historic traditions of their craft in a changing world. The officials of the Garment Workers, on the other hand, are, with few exceptions, filled with a zeal to break down the existing economic structure. Whereas most of the employers speak warmly of the moderation and common-sense of the A.S.T. & T., it is hard to find one among them who will utter a good word for the members of the other Union with whom they come in official contact. Perhaps even more outspoken are the criticisms levelled by the leaders of the two Unions at each other. " Fifty years behind the times," " A mere stumbling-block in the way of progress," grumbles the T. & G.W.T.U. about the A.S.T. & T., to which the latter replies, " A pack of hot-heads who will bring the industry to no good," " A mob of ignorant agitators." So bitter has the feeling been that co-operation in the furtherance of mutual interest has become well-nigh impossible in recent years. This is even true of the West End branches, where the members are in each case handicraft tailors, and where the Garment Workers' branch officials are of a somewhat different calibre from those in other parts of the country.

It has, in fact, been in the West End of London that the two Unions have most frequently come to blows. The trouble began in 1905, when many of the members of the West End branch of the A.S.T. & T., resenting the control of their activities exercised by the head office of the Union in Manchester, organized a " Home Rule for London " campaign, which ended in their secession from the A.S.T. & T. and the formation of a separate Union—" The London Society of Tailors and Tailoresses." For several years after this event, though bitterness and bad feeling were accumulating, no outward breach of the peace between the new society and the parent body took place. Agreements with the employers' organization about log-rates and other matters, which had previously been negotiated by the A.S.T. & T. were now framed at meetings at which both bodies were represented. Generally speaking, however, the younger Union was inclined to go the further in its demands. A crisis finally came in 1912. The London Society demanded a revision of the log and an increase of 2d. per hour in log-rates. Without so much as consulting the leaders of the A.S.T. & T. it called its men out on strike, after a mere show of negotiation with the employers. Many of the A.S.T. & T. men went out at the same time— against the wishes of their local committee, and particularly in flagrant disregard of the advice of the Executive at Manchester. After six weeks' struggle, the strike came to an unsuccessful close and the London Society found itself with depleted funds and with every prospect of dissolving into thin air.[1] At this juncture the secretary approached the Leeds Union, which was later to become known as the United Garment Workers' Trade Union, and which, besides having already two branches among the factory operatives in the East End, was about this time trying to organize a new London branch of cutters. After protracted negotiations an amalgamation was arranged in 1915, and the " London Society of Tailors and Tailoresses " became known as the London (West End) branch of the " United Garment Workers' Trade Union." Whether its members meet with a readier appreciation of their local

---

[1] The leading figure in this disastrous dispute was Mr Tom Mann.

problems at Leeds than they did, prior to 1905, at Manchester, is at least doubtful. If we may believe their branch secretary, they are not even allowed to spend money on the hire of a hall for a branch meeting without special authorization from headquarters.

From this time forward the local squabbles in London were merged in the growing antagonism between the A.S.T. & T. and the U.G.W.T.U., which was developing throughout the country. A further chapter was written in 1921, again in consequence of a hastily-called strike, to which the A.S.T. & T. was only an unwilling party. The following account of what occurred is mainly derived from the pages of the A.S.T. & T.'s journal, but it is believed that allowance has been made for the natural bias displayed in that quarter. The trouble began with a proposal from the Association of London Master Tailors (representing the retail employers of the West End) that the two Unions should discuss with them the best means to be adopted "with a view to relieving unemployment." This meant, in effect, a proposal to reduce wages. When the detailed proposals were put before the Union representatives, the latter agreed, after some hesitation, to consult their membership before making a definite reply. From the workers' point of view, joint action between the two Unions at this stage was clearly essential, but the friction between them was so great that when, a fortnight later, the employers asked for a reply, no joint meeting had actually taken place. After another week the employers met again and agreed amongst themselves on a reduced scale of log-rates, to come into force within four days if in the meantime no agreement should be arrived at with the Trade Unions. Though on this occasion the employers' secretary did all he could to facilitate joint action by the two Unions, the latter still failed to present a united front.

On the day after the new rates came into force, both Unions, meeting separately, decided to call out their men. During the next six weeks repeated attempts were made to arrive at a settlement, but in no case was it found possible to devise a schedule of wage-reductions to which both the Unions, as well as the employers, could agree. When, after much delay, a joint committee of the Unions was convened to deal with picketing and other matters, the Executive of the Garment Workers' Union at Leeds promptly refused to authorize this joint action. Encouraged by this internal weakness in the workers' camp, the employers gradually stiffened their terms. In the end, after nearly two months' unemployment during what is normally the busiest time of the year, the workers had to go back at rates considerably less favourable than had been offered them, and refused by one or other of the Unions, at an earlier stage of the dispute.

Similar stories of internecine feuds can be told of other parts of the country, and more especially of Ireland, where, in consequence, a Union membership which at one time reached a figure of 10,000 or 12,000 has now sunk to insignificant proportions. The story here is briefly as follows : During the war the A.S.T. & T., which had always had a fairly strong membership among Irish handicraft tailors, and which had for some time taken an interest in the conditions of the totally unorganized factory- and home-workers in the Shirt and Collar trade in the north, succeeded in enrolling some 10,000 Irish factory members, of whom about half were in Derry. Shortly afterwards the T. & G.W.T.U., which had hitherto been sublimely indifferent to Irish affairs, appeared on the scene and organized a strike among the shirt-cutters in Derry, promising to secure for them an increase in wages of 15s. per week. Those immediately concerned only numbered 200, but in consequence of the stoppage many thousands (including the five thousand members of the A.S.T. & T.) were thrown out of work. Neither the latter Union nor the local Trades'

Council gave any encouragement to the strikers, whose demands they regarded as unreasonable ; the employers were able to get most of their urgent work done by their own branch factories in England or Scotland ; and after serious disturbances, in consequence of which the city was occupied by the military, the strike came to an untimely end. In the result the A.S.T. & T., in spite of heroic efforts to retain its members by the expenditure of over £4000 in supporting those thrown involuntarily out of work, was left with its organization completely smashed. Ultimately the T. & G.W.T.U. had the melancholy satisfaction of enrolling a few hundred members in the district, and of knowing that among Irish factory workers it was now the only Union in the field; a satisfaction, however, which it must have found hard to reconcile with any real desire to improve industrial conditions in the Shirt and Collar trade.

While this central feud goes on from year to year, a certain undercurrent of hostility is also noticeable between the A.S.T. & T. and the T. & G.W.T.U. on the one hand and the various other bodies having clothing operatives in their ranks on the other. Of these latter the National Union of General Workers, the Shop Assistants' Union, and the National Union of Distributive and Allied Workers are the most important. The two former naturally do not come into contact to any considerable extent with the A.S.T. & T., since the one only enrols the less skilled workers and the other the employees in the dressmaking, millinery and mantle workshops of department stores and other retailers ; but the N.U.D.A.W. includes a fair number of tailors working for co-operative stores and is accordingly regarded by the craft union with no little hostility. In the same way the T. & G.W.T.U. resents the intrusion of the general unions in what it not unjustifiably regards as its own special field. This attitude would be even more reasonable if the Garment Workers could lay any claim to success in organizing the whole of the clothing industry. As it is, there is little doubt that most of the Shop Assistants' and General Workers' membership in the sewing trades consists of women who would otherwise be totally unorganized. In view of this it would seem that the T. & G.W.T.U.'s hostility is inspired by jealousy as much as by any other motive.

Various attempts have been made at one time or another to form special unions of cutters, none of which have met with any marked success. One of the principal difficulties has been the fact that, while a great many cutters are mere employees in large factories, and as such eligible for membership of the Garment Workers' Trade Union, and often enthusiastic members of it, at the other end of the scale the interests of a cutter at a fashionable tailoring establishment are almost indistinguishable from those of his employer, with whom, in fact, he may even aspire to go into partnership. In between there lies a large body whose interests are rather indeterminate. It is among men of this type that a " Cutters' Union " was formed a few years ago at Liverpool, and gradually spread out into several local branches, partly aided in this expansion by the suggestion then current that a " Distributive Workers' " Trade Board might be established, in which event, of course, it would prove desirable from the cutters' point of view that they should have some definite body to voice their interests. The same possibility induced perhaps 150 cutters in different parts of the country to join the Shop Assistants' Union. Altogether there are probably some 4500 cutters in retail shops who would be eligible for membership of a union of this type, in addition to the 4500 in the factories, who are unlikely to join any body but the T. & G.W.T.U. When it later on became obvious that there was no immediate likelihood of any extension of the Trade Board system to the distributive trades, the popularity of trade unionism among cutters underwent an eclipse. It must be added that there are various bodies, such as the "United Kingdom Association of Foremen Cutters," whose members are all cutters of one sort or another, but these societies are all either Friendly Societies or technical associations, whose activities comprise such things as the production of technical journals, and are devoid of any political or industrial significance.

Before leaving the subject of trade unionism, it may be interesting to consider on what lines future developments are likely to take place. For this purpose the A.S.T. & T. may reasonably be omitted from consideration. It is unlikely to increase in size or even to maintain its present numbers. Indeed, on various occasions the question of an amalgamation between it and the T. & G.W.T.U. has been raised, and the fusion would probably ere now have taken place if it had not been for the clash of personalities involved. In general it may be said that it has been the A.S.T. & T. which has stood out, but this will not be surprising to one who is aware of the opinion its leaders hold of the men at the head of the other Union. Whatever may be thought of the thorny problem of craft *versus* industrial unionism, it is obviously unreasonable that there should exist, as there do, two bodies competing in the same field and constantly overlapping, so that, for instance, the Scottish handicraft tailors are members of the Tailors' and Garment Workers' Trade Union while the factory operatives in Kettering owe allegiance to the Amalgamated Society of Tailors and Tailoresses. If, and when, fusion comes, it may be desirable to maintain separate branches for the handicraft tailors in the larger towns, as is done to-day in London and Glasgow by the T. & G.W.T.U., but that is another question. If there is no fusion, the A.S.T. & T. will probably occupy a progressively less important place beside the T. & G.W.T.U., as the latter body gradually expands so as to embrace the entire industry on the factory side—as there is every reason to suppose it will one day do.

Future policy, then, rests mainly in the hands of the larger

Union. In estimating what it is likely to be, we should be unwise to look for clues in the Union's past history. During the years of its most striking growth, the brain on which the Union has mainly relied has been that of Mr. J. J. Mallon, well-known as the Warden of Toynbee Hall and the most ardent supporter of the Trade Board system, for the parentage of which in this country he can in fact claim a large share of the credit. In order that there might be some organization to which he could turn to put forward names for the workers' sides of the Trade Boards created in the clothing industries immediately after the war, Mr Mallon successfully urged the U.G.W.T.U. to attempt the organization, not only of the workers in the wholesale tailoring trades, but of all and sundry, home-workers as well as factory-workers, in any branch of the clothing industry. The sudden adoption of this policy, which has, as we have seen, been by no means as yet entirely successful, meant inevitably that a good many hot-heads came to the fore in the counsels of the union. Just after the war a number of rather foolish strikes were embarked on, and the most Utopian programmes received approval from the leaders —the complete abolition of piece-work, for instance, and a minimum wage (in 1924) of £4 a week for adult male employees. In London, in particular, whence most of the newly-enrolled members were drawn, wild ideas were prevalent, and much nonsense was talked, which served no purpose but to antagonize the more reasonable employers.

With the decline of membership in recent years, a new outlook seems to be emerging. The strikes, for instance, began to be more scientifically planned. Instead of calling a general strike of all clothing workers in a given locality, special firms, where abuses have been alleged to exist, have been singled out, —in Leicester, in Hackney, in Southwark and elsewhere—and improved payment or conditions have been secured. This policy recalls that pursued by the A.S.T. & T. in its early days, which we have already described. It must be added that it has latterly been defeated in the same manner in which the A.S.T. & T.'s campaign was defeated—namely, by the intervention of the employers' association, in this case "The Wholesale Clothing Manufacturers' Federation," with the threat of a general lock-out. Another recent development has been seen in the increased efforts which have been made to reach friendly local agreements with employers in various districts. It has been proposed at one time or another to move the offices of the Union to London, and when this takes place, as it undoubtedly will, one important source of instability will have been removed. At present, the local officials in London, being subordinate to the Executive in Leeds, and at the same time chafing under this subordination, are apt to act irresponsibly. This is true of both the East and West End branches. It is anomalous that the headquarters of an important industry, of which the metropolis is the principal centre, should be situated in a provincial town, even a town so important from the industry's point of view as Leeds.

On the whole, it is safe to predict a more constructive and less turbulent policy than has been pursued in the past. There are many important problems which a union speaking for a large majority of the workers will have to face. Methods of remuneration, means of reducing seasonal unemployment, the provision of workshop accommodation in the West End, schemes for extending the subdivisional system to the handicraft tailoring trade, schemes for overcoming the present shortage of apprentices—all these things will have to be considered and will only be satisfactorily dealt with by hard thinking on the part of men imbued with an adequate sense of responsibility. That such men will be forthcoming there can be little doubt. Trade unionists have learned some very important and necessary lessons since the days when they first began to feel themselves to be a power in the land.

K

CHAPTER VII

EMPLOYERS' ASSOCIATIONS

WITH the growth in the strength of the workers' unions has proceeded a corresponding extension of organization among the employers. In the one case, as in the other, the inauguration of the Trade Boards system has considerably hastened development. As soon as manufacturers became aware of the fact that matters closely affecting their interests were being settled by bodies in the election of which they could only take part as members of employers' associations, they naturally hastened to enrol in those associations which existed already or to take part in the formation of new ones. It has thus come about that the chief function of the employers' associations has been to conduct negotiations with the workers, both through the medium of the Trade Boards, and, in some cases, by direct negotiation with the trade union officials. In most cases, however, some attention is paid to other matters of general interest to the section of the trade concerned. The London employers' association, for instance, has devoted much consideration to the means of meeting foreign competition in the home market, while the National Federation of Merchant Tailors interests itself in schemes for extending subdivisional methods to handicraft tailoring.

Employers' associations can be most easily classified along the same lines as those usually adopted in classifying the various sections of the industry. In the handicraft section of the retail trade the most important body is the Association of London Master Tailors, representing Bond Street and Hanover

Square. The rest of the trade is catered for by the National Federation of Merchant Tailors, a body with branches throughout the country, which, however, has not yet succeeded in winning the allegiance of more than 5 per cent. of those who might become members. The Jewish subcontractors are represented by the Master Tailors' Association, with members in many large towns, but with its principal strength in East and West London. The women's retail trades in London are provided for by the London Employers' Association, a recently formed but powerful organization which dominates the employers' sides of the Trade Boards in the field it represents. In the wholesale trades, the only really important association is the Wholesale Clothing Manufacturers' Federation of Great Britain. The women's wholesale trades are scarcely represented by any employers' association worth considering.

The Association of London Master Tailors covers the cream of the West End tailoring trade and includes about 100 out of perhaps 300 retail tailors in West and Central London. It has been in existence for over forty years and is the counterpart of the West End branches of the A.S.T. & T. and the T. & G.W.T.U., with which bodies it has periodical conferences to settle disputed points in connection with the London log. This system of piece-work payment was agreed to in its present form by a conference held in 1891, though minor modifications have since been introduced. In the Constitution of the A.L.M.T. the objects of the Association are declared to be :

(a) The *mutual protection* of its members.

(b) The *interchange of information* on matters connected with the Trade.

(c) To provide for *friendly communication* with the representatives of the workmen, with a view to the *settlement*, by arbitration or otherwise, of any dispute or grievance that affects the Trade.

It is further provided in the Rules that " every member of the Association pay the wages of his work-people in accordance with the London Time-log for piece-work recognized by the Association and registered at the Board of Trade and Ministry of Labour . . . or at its accepted equivalent rate per Working Clock hour. . . ." The first of the objects above enumerated is provided for by a benevolent fund for members of the Association. This is administered by a separate body under the style of the Master Tailors' Benevolent Association, and has aroused much jealousy among members of the National Federation of Merchant Tailors, who roundly assert that it is the sole *raison d'être* of the Association, and that but for it West End tailors would be willing to merge their own Association in the N.F.M.T. In point of fact the other objects of the Constitution are regarded by the A.L.M.T. as being of equal importance. The maintenance of their supremacy is aided by constant interchange of information and by steady and, on the whole, successful efforts to enlist the goodwill of the workers. Until, at least, the N.F.M.T. imposes on its own members the adoption of the London log, which it is extremely unlikely to do, it is useless for it to indulge hopes of absorbing the A.L.M.T. This point was driven home in a letter written by Mr Cooling Lawrence, the President of the Association, to the Committee of the N.F.M.T. in June 1924, in which he stated that " as an Association the A.L.M.T. exists solely for dealing with log-rates and wages, and is not interested in any outside matters."

The National Federation of Merchant Tailors was founded in the provinces about twenty years ago, mainly as a means of countering the A.S.T. & T.'s policy of singling out special towns for strike action, which has been described in the last chapter. It aims at including all the leading establishments in the trade ; but being definitely an *association of employers*, it does not cater for the small man who works (either alone or with a few

employees) direct for his customers. At present the membership amounts only to about 2000 out of the 30,000 tailors whom
the Association would like to see enrolled. In the *Merchant
Tailor*, the monthly organ of the Federation, it was stated in
January 1924 that members were falling off rapidly, though
the tide seems now to have been stemmed. Branches of the
Association are to be found everywhere, but its main strength
is now in London, where the central offices are situated in a
commodious building in Hanover Square. From a brief
perusal of the pages of the *Merchant Tailor* a very fair idea of
the chief activities of the Federation can be gleaned. Owing
to its comparative weakness, except in a very few provincial
towns where it has won the allegiance of, say, 90 per cent. of
the local retail tailors, it cannot claim to speak as a really
representative body for the purpose of wage negotiations,
though, in the London area and elsewhere, it does take part
in these, and is represented on the Retail Tailoring Trade
Board. Its leading activities are of a different order. Prominent
among them are those of a social character, including frequent
dinners, as well as the Annual Conference, generally held in a
town or seaside resort whence a variety of char-à-banc expedi-
tions can be arranged. A fair amount of propaganda work is
carried on. This includes, on the one hand, a campaign against
the Trade Board rates, and, on the other hand, a constant
guerrilla warfare against tailoring establishments which, while
claiming to turn out hand-made suits, do in fact patronize
wholesale bespoke factories without acknowledging it. The
anti-Trade-Board campaign is only one symptom of a
general resentment of Government interference, whether it
takes the form of wage regulation or of the extension of
the Factory Code to retailers' workshops. In his address
to the Annual Conference at Blackpool in October 1924, the
Chairman spoke as follows : " Ours is a peaceful policy
so long as we are permitted to conduct our business as we

desire, but militant if we are faced with Government or other outside interference which threatens our interest. As regards the Trade Boards, I consider it our duty to try to secure relief." In the same month a prominent member delivered a long tirade at the Hanover Square offices against the Labour Government's Factories Bill of 1924, from which the following are extracts : " Every reasonable employer affords washing facilities for his workers and seats for the female workers, and there is little hardship in the worst type of employer being obliged to do these things. But it is in extending the power of the Home Secretary that the Bill is important. The powers of the Factory Inspectors are considerably increased, and in many cases no appeal can be made against the Inspectors' decisions ; and there is an attempt to limit, by a Parliamentary Bill, the hours of labour of adult male workers. . . . First, the distinctions between factories and workshops are abolished, so that every tailor's workroom or workshop becomes a factory, whether it is in London or in a country village. In factories, in the past, there has always been a higher standard of requirements than in workshops ; but that is now to cease and the high standard will, if the Bill is not altered, be enforced in the workshops. And not merely this, but the standard is to be raised higher than ever before.

" Under the Bill, the air-space for each person is increased from 250 cubic feet to 400 feet and no height over 14 feet can be reckoned in. Further, the Home Secretary will have power to raise this statutory requirement even higher. Few employers will object to a First Aid outfit being provided by them, and kept in a workshop ; but this Bill will give the Home Secretary the power to require special medical provision for the workers whenever he sees fit. . . . The resolutions of the Washington Convention are greatly restrictive in character, and in adopting them we (Great Britain) are handicapping ourselves in the stern competition in business that is likely to come. . . . The hours of work question should not be dealt with as a side issue in a Bill called a Factory Bill. With a Sunday rest we are all in agreement, but a limit of a 48-hour week to women workers will limit the time of employment of adult men to similar hours in many cases. . . . We are being governed more and more by departmental control, and the powers of the Inspectors are barely understood, even by the Inspectors themselves. We do not want arbitrary interference in the conduct of our businesses. In the past an employer could lodge objections to any regulations proposed by the Home Secretary as a matter of right ; but under the Bill the right is taken away, and a public enquiry can only be demanded by a majority of employers, such as our Federation ; for unless this Bill is altered, no individual employer has even the right to say a word in defence of his industry.

"The transferring of the powers that used to be exercised by the Sanitary Inspectors to the Factory Inspectors means that the right of appeal to a magistrate will disappear in many cases, and the arbitrary decision of the Inspectors will be final. . . . At present we may say that workshops are graded according to the purpose for which they are used ; but the grading will disappear in the new Bill and the same high standard will be required in all of them. In many cases where a District Council hesitates to prosecute, the Bill will give power to the Factory Inspector to prosecute. . . . It is not certain how our workers will like some of the new conditions, for the new Clause 57 prohibits spitting on the floor of a workshop if the occupier puts up a notice to that effect. . . . New Clause 58 states that underground or more than half underground workrooms may be closed if the Inspector considers them unsuitable for the purpose ; and this Section applies to the tailoring industry. The room may be closed as unsuitable in construction, light, ventilation or in any other respect, which is rather indefinite. . . . Clause 45 will prevent your men from working in your own workshop on Saturdays after 6 o'clock, or on Sundays ; but they may work in their own homes and employ members of their families at these times. . . ."

The foregoing lengthy quotation has been inserted because it typifies the attitude of the average employer to any sort or form of government interference with his industry. With the specific question of the fairness or otherwise of the Trade Board rates, especially as they affect learners and apprentices, we deal elsewhere.

With regard to the attitude of members of the N.F.M.T. towards their fellow-retailers, we reproduce a few samples of the complaints which the Federation has made about unfair methods of trade. One of the constantly recurring complaints is that many retail tailors patronize subcontractors. " Many of the ' bargain ' firms do their business with the aid of sub-contractors of the ' Cut, Make and Trim ' type ; and others by arrangement with clothing manufacturers. This means that they themselves do no single item of the operations incidental to production. They merely book the order and deliver the goods ; some other concern does the rest. Any retail trader could do the same." The writer then goes on to suggest that members of the N.F.M.T. should follow suit ! Another common accusation is that much of the advertising of cheap clothing is misleading. " There is not the slightest doubt that those who apply the term ' tailor-made ' to every description of factory-made clothing want to convey to the public the impression that their goods are made by journeymen tailors and are equal in quality to clothing really made by the latter, though the price quoted for it is far below that at which genuine tailoring can be profitably supplied. . . . So glaring is the misuse of the term in numberless cases that one fails to see how the law dealing with the misdescription of goods cannot be brought to bear on them. It ought to be subject to similar penalties to those imposed when margarine is sold as butter. . . . We

have heard a good deal of late about ' truth in advertising,'
but I venture to say that nowhere are so many untruths
allowed to go unchecked as in certain sections of the tailoring
trades. . . . In one of the London dailies there appeared an
advertisement of a firm announcing the ' phenomenal offer '
of a best quality worsted suiting, tailor-made in best West
End style, and all the gush with which these advertisements
are usually offered to the unsuspecting public, the price of a
suit being £3, 3s. A customer of mine, out of curiosity, wrote
for patterns of the worsteds as advertised, and in reply he
received a selection of cheap Yorkshire tweeds which by no
stretch of the imagination bore out the high-sounding claims
which were made for them. . . ." In this connection it is
interesting to note that the Sheffield branch of the N.F.M.T.
publishes periodical advertisements in the local newspapers
reproducing the certificate of membership of the Federation
and urging the general public who may be needing the services
of legitimate bespoke tailors " to look for the sign as a guarantee
of reliability and quality." With the airing of another grievance many of us will feel full sympathy. " The system of
' touting ' outside shops, which is largely indulged in by many
so-called ' tailors,' is becoming an intolerable nuisance in many
of the busiest and most important streets in London. The
public resents the obtrusive and objectionable methods of
the ' touts,' and it is bringing the tailoring trade into disrepute.
The most casual passing glance at a shop-window is sufficient
to cause one of the pests to pounce upon you. If you pause to
look at the alluring displays, one of them will spot you and
stick to you like a leech."

Another class of people with whom the N.F.M.T. concerns
itself is the woollen manufacturers. Some of the subjects it
discusses with the Woollen Merchants' Association are questions
of who should pay carriage on orders, of discounts, of a proper
standard of Indigo and other dyes, of their durability,

and, in particular, of unfair selling of cloth " direct to the customer." [1]

Finally, the N.F.M.T. has been displaying of late years considerable anxiety about the decay of apprenticeship, and besides pressing for vocational training in Day Schools has prepared schemes for the dilution of skilled labour by the adoption of a limited degree of team-work, or, as they prefer to call it, "reinforced labour," which they claim does not result in the loss of individuality commonly associated with sub-divisional systems. These were the subject of a leading article in the *Merchant Tailor* in January 1924. " Unhappily owing to want of forethought and neglect of trade interest, the easier way of resorting to subcontracting and other methods was adopted, resulting in the present shortage of skilled labour and absence of effective methods of training. For some considerable time there has been a growing desire among the members of the N.F.M.T. that an attempt should be made to regularize the methods of production, rearranging the one-man-one-garment system which has prevailed for so long, utilizing the newer method of dilution of labour, so as to preserve the best and most efficient points in the individual system, and at the same time enabling the workers to increase their production without any decrease in their earnings. . . . A special subcommittee of practical men has been formed ; the various methods of making garments compared ; tests instituted with average workers, and finally a scheme of dilution was prepared suitable for the workrooms of all better-class employers. It was steadily kept in view that excellence of workmanship rather than cheapening of cost must be the first consideration. The scheme provides for a combination of three, five or ten workers and is capable of expansion if required. Specification of garments, particulars of division, and results obtained by each combination of workers is given ; also the

[1] See *Merchant Tailor*, p, 208, June 1924.

application of dilution to vests and trousers is included. . . .
To meet the growing requirements of many members who,
owing to difficulties of obtaining a sufficient supply of skilled
workers, have been compelled to resort to the subcontractor
and other sources, it is proposed that one or more pioneer
workshops be started capable of turning out, say, 500 suits
and other garments per week."

It is a little difficult to see how the workshops referred to
in the above passage differ materially from those of a subcontractor. In fact, the scheme appears to consist in establishing a series of subcontracting houses, the shareholders in
which are members of the N.F.M.T. There is also a suggestion
that it will enable experiments in regard to subdivisional
methods and dilution of labour to be carried out, but how far
the promoters are actuated by a scientific interest in their
trade and how far by jealousy of their more successful competitors is doubtful. Further particulars of the scheme may
be gleaned from the following further passage : " It is evident
that if the new Factories Bill (of 1924) becomes a law, many
tailors will have to consider whether it is still worth while to
run their own workshops. . . . Under the scheme of the
Federation, we are endeavouring to obtain the best machinery,
and get into touch with the most skilled operatives, and pay
prices which will induce them to stay with the Company. The
main object is to produce tailoring of the highest class on the
best and most scientific principles. Subdivisional workshops
have undoubtedly come to stay. There are those who are
running subdivisional workshops and doing fairly well out of
them. Surely what the middleman is doing can be done by
the merchant tailor.

" Of the £2000 capital required more than half has been
subscribed " (this was in 1924). . . . " The first workshop will
be situated in London, and in time branches will be established
throughout the country as they are required. . . . Share-

holders will, of course, have first attention, secondly members of the Federation. Outsiders' work will at certain times be welcomed, but they cannot expect to have the same advantages as shareholders, especially during the busy season." Since the above was written, the Company has been established under the title of " The Federation General Workshops Company, Limited."

The Master Tailors' Association is composed exclusively of subcontractors, and almost, though not entirely, of Jews. In London it comprises about 600 out of a possible 1600 members, though the exact membership fluctuates considerably. In the provinces its chief strength is in Manchester, Glasgow, Liverpool, Birmingham, Leeds, Sheffield, and Nottingham, in the above order. It also has a few members in nearly every large town where subcontractors are to be found. Unlike the N.F.M.T. it is more concerned with negotiations about wages and prices than about any other matters. It is represented on the employers' side of the Wholesale Bespoke Tailoring Trade Board, but, as the average subcontractor pays wages in excess of Trade Board rates, the main interest of its members lies almost more in maintaining the prices received by the subcontractor from the retailer than in attempts to whittle down wage-rates.

On the retail side of the women's light clothing trades, the only important federation of employers is to be found in London under the title of the London Employers' Association. This body was formed in 1918 as the outcome of a committee of leading London drapers and department stores which had for some time previously been in existence for the purpose of making agreements with the trade unions in which the employees in their workshops were organized. The conclusion of such agreements is still the Association's principal function ; and those now current include agreements with the A.S.T. & T., the T. & G.W,T.U., the Shop Assistants' Union (Metropolitan

Needlework Section), and the National Union of General Workers (Women Workers' Section), and relate to hours, wages and conditions in the Retail Bespoke Tailoring section (separate agreements for male and female workers), the Wholesale Dressmaking and Women's Light Clothing section, the Retail Dressmaking section and the Millinery section. In some cases the wages agreed on are above the Trade Board rates; and among the other matters dealt with are overtime-rates, provision for payment on Bank holidays, for annual weekly holidays on full-pay, for the supply of tea, and of dining-room accommodation, for the opening of the premises at 8 A.M. to provide shelter for girls who travel by workmen's trams or trains, for the avoidance, if possible, of short time, for punctuality on the part of the workers, etc., etc. The Association dominates the employers' side on the Dressmaking and Women's Light Clothing (England and Wales), the Hat, Cap and Millinery (England and Wales), and the Ostrich Feather Trade Boards. In the case of each of the above Boards the secretary of the employers' side is the general secretary of the L.E.A.

Another phase of the Association's activities relates to the recruitment of young workers, in which connection it works in close contact with Juvenile Advisory Committees and with Head-masters' and Head-mistresses' Committees, through whom it obtains suitable candidates for employment as clerks and saleswomen as well as in the dressmaking workshops.

Much attention has also been paid to the development of overseas markets and to methods of meeting foreign competition in the home market. Statistics of imports and exports are compiled and circulated to members, together with occasional memoranda on matters of topical interest, of which the following is an example: " December 5th, 1924. The policy of our Association is ' business for the British employer ' and, what necessarily follows, ' work for the British worker.' We make no complaint about the foreign firm which comes to this country and opens an establishment and contributes to the rates and taxes in the same way as the British employer, but we intend to do everything in our power to prevent orders going abroad at the expense of the British employer and worker, to firms who temporarily plant themselves at our hotels or at the house of some distinguished hostess, and by doing so avoid all taxation and overhead charges to which our employers are subject. The policy adopted by certain society ladies in inviting French dressmakers to display models at their London houses—and this at a time when many British dressmaking firms are finding it difficult to obtain sufficient orders to keep their workers employed—cannot be too strongly condemned. It should also be borne in mind that some of these ladies are the wives of our leading public men, and while the husband is professing his concern about unemployment from the political platform, his wife is doing all she can to foster foreign trade at the expense of our own employers and workers.

" Another aspect of the case is worth drawing attention to : This Association believes in the payment of reasonable rates of wages and good conditions of employment, for the workers employed by its members. Collective bargaining with the Trade Unions has been our declared policy ever since the Association came into being, and at the present time our members are observing an agreement which provides for higher rates for competent workers than those fixed by the Trade Board, and payment at the rate of time-and-a-half for any overtime work, in addition to which the conditions of employment include payment for Bank and Summer holidays, a maximum 48-hour working week, and in many cases tea is provided. The French employer has no Trade Board determinations to comply with, and is free to pay such rates of wages as he may think fit, and it is common knowledge that the French worker is not paid at anything like the rates obtaining in London, added to which the hours worked are invariably longer."

Turning now to the wholesale trades, we find in the tailoring section a powerful Association—the Wholesale Clothing Manufacturers' Federation of Great Britain. Nearly all the Wholesale Clothing firms are members of this body, or of one of the local associations affiliated to it, such as the Northern Clothing Manufacturers' Association of Leeds and the Huddersfield Clothiers' Association. The chief exceptions are provided by the wholesale firms which sell direct to the public through their own retail shops, and which, for this reason, are ineligible for membership. The Federation appoints most of the members of the employers' side of the Ready-made and Wholesale Bespoke Trade Board. It is regarded with considerable hostility by the trade unions, with whom it conducts negotiations outside as well as within the Trade Board. It also deals with some other matters of interest to the trade, especially in connection with the terms on which transactions with cloth manufacturers on the one hand, and retailers on the other, are conducted. Full information about its activities is difficult to come by, as its members do not court publicity.

In all other factory sections of the clothing trades, the employers are badly organized. A variety of bodies, national and local, exists, and though many of them are represented on the Trade Boards, the influence they exert is slight compared with that wielded by the Wholesale Clothing Manufacturers' Federation in its own field. One of the most important is the Shirt and Collar Federation, which covers the bulk of the employers in that trade and whose representatives are the chief spokesmen of the employers on the Shirt Trade Board. Among the local bodies, the Yorkshire Blouse, Overall, and Underclothing Manufacturers' Association, with headquarters at Leeds, and largely inspired by the interesting personality of

Mr T. M. Heron, is worth mentioning. So is the Making-up trade section of the Nottingham Chamber of Commerce, which exerts in Nottingham an influence comparable with that of the London Employers' Association in London. The British Wholesale Mantles and Costumes Manufacturers, with headquarters in London, the Birmingham Ladies' and Children's Clothing Manufacturers' Association, the British Corset Makers, the Wholesale Hat and Cap Manufacturers, the Ladies' and Children's Clothing (Manchester) Manufacturers' Association and the London Blouse, Underclothing and Allied Manufacturers' Association are the names of a few other employers' organizations in the women's trades. None of them, however, is of sufficient importance to warrant more detailed discussion of its activities.

CHAPTER VIII

APPRENTICESHIP AND THE PROBLEM OF RECRUITMENT

ONE of the most serious problems facing the more skilled sections of the Clothing Trades to-day is the complete breakdown of the methods of recruitment by which new workers have in the past been obtained. On this point there is unanimous agreement. In 1922, for instance, a deputation from the Bedford Master Tailors' Association informed Mr Kellaway, M.P., that in Bedford, a town of 40,000 inhabitants, there were only three female learners and no male learners in the tailoring trade. The President of the National Federation of Merchant Tailors, at the Annual Meeting of that body at Blackpool in September 1924, spoke to the same effect : " The supply of skilled labour in our trade is drying up. Efforts are being made to improve the supply by making it possible for the art of tailoring to be taught to boys before leaving school. . . . We have the support of the workers (*i.e.* ' The Amalgamated Society of Tailors and Tailoresses ')." The editor of the *Merchant Tailor* expresses himself a little more fully : " In recent years the village apprentice has disappeared. The majority of the skilled tailors in the workshops of the tailoring trade, in all the large cities to-day, received their early training in the craft in the small village establishments or accompanying the ' itinerant journeyman ' (referred to in the first chapter). The small Master Tailor was an individual upon whom we depended for the rough material which we licked into shape in the larger workshops in the towns and cities. That source is rapidly drying up, and the supply of skilled tailors is in

L

consequence inadequate even to-day to meet the demands of the trade. One factor—*but by no means the only factor*[1]— responsible for the depletion of the apprenticeship ranks was the introduction of the Trade Board system of a recent date, with its flat rate of payment for general application. Gradually the country trades began to drop the taking on of apprentices because of the prohibitive wage-rates, rates which, though probably an economic proposition in the towns, were out of all proportion in the rural districts. A result of this has been to introduce into the sewing end of the craft a greater proportion of female help, and this proportion is gradually on the increase, and it is not difficult to contemplate the time—unless something unforeseen happens in the meantime—when nearly all the actual making of the garments will be in the hands of the female workers and only a few men tailors will be left to do the supervising and pressing." There may be disagreement about the contention that the decay of apprenticeship has been caused by the Trade Boards Act ; of that hereafter. But as to the fact of its decay all speak with one accord.

Complaints similar to the foregoing first made themselves heard about twenty-five years ago, and during the past fifteen have grown steadily more frequent and emphatic. Most commonly they refer to handicraft tailoring. A similar state of affairs, however, prevails in the subdivisional section ; and in any branch of the industry which requires skilled hands. In this respect, indeed, the clothing trades are not in a class by themselves, but share in a peculiarly notable degree the problems of recruitment which face most of our skilled industries.

A consideration of the decay of apprenticeship among handicraft tailors naturally divides itself into two parts. We have in the first place to note what is certainly the permanent disappearance of the village tailors, in whose shops the great bulk of the apprentices formerly served their time. Secondly,

[1] Italics mine.

in view of the drying up of this source of supply, we must enquire the reasons why the tailors who still carry on business in the large towns have not made good the deficiency by training their own apprentices. With regard to the first of these points, it is urged by employers that the responsibility lies primarily with the Trade Board rates. " Apprentices have in the main been trained by the village tailors, and it is on these unfortunate traders that the flat (*i.e.* Trade Boards) rate has fallen most heavily, and I say advisedly that it is an unjust rate so far as the village tailor is concerned, because it practically takes his life out his hands and crushes him out of existence. It is the village tailor who takes the rough material and trains it into the workers who become the skilled workers in city workshops. . . . In the large towns, owing to the conditions of labour, we have not trained enough apprentices even to supply the wastage. . . . It is not good for the nation that people should be divorced from their natural surroundings and pursuits, or that an old industry should be crushed out of existence." How far, if at all, the blame lies with the Trade Board rates it is a little difficult to say. It is at least arguable that the little village tailors, who have undoubtedly been having a bad time, have become an uneconomic factor. In the past, their clientele has mainly consisted of the middle and lower-middle classes. The cut of the clothes they turned out and the range of patterns which they kept in stock was never such as to satisfy really well-to-do people, who have always patronized the West End, or at the very least, the neighbouring county or cathedral town. The agricultural labourer, on the other hand, has for a long time past been clothed in garments produced in the wholesale clothing factories. Now it is precisely to the middle and lower-middle classes that the suits now being made on the wholesale bespoke system, and being sold, as often as not by the chain-store type of clothing manufacturer, in ever-increasing quantities, make their chief appeal. Crippled by the competition of giant businesses which, besides outbidding him in up-to-dateness of style and range of choice, can also afford to undersell him, the village tailor cannot hope to survive. That the wage-rates fixed by the Trade Boards with their eyes on the urban conditions for adult workers no less than for apprentices, have hastened the process of his extinction, need scarcely be disputed, but this must be regarded as a contributory and not as a main cause.

If this is so, it may be asked, how is it that the trade in London and elsewhere has not frankly recognized the fact that it will in future have to be self-supporting in regard to its labour supply ? There can be little doubt that the most important reason is to be found in the bad conditions under which handicraft tailors live and work, the long months of unemployment or under-employment they have in the off-seasons to endure, and the consequent reluctance they feel in bringing up their children to follow their own trade ; for, as in other industries, it is from tailors' families that new tailors must in the main be recruited if they are to be recruited at all. It is remarkable that even among employers this view is not seriously disputed, though other causes are held to have almost equal weight. It must be remembered that the handicraft tailor is, to some extent, an independent craftsman, not uncommonly working for more than one employer, and seldom employed on the retailer's premises. The apprentice, therefore, where he exists, is indentured to the working tailor and not to the owner of the retail shop who employs him. For this reason the employers do not feel directly to blame for the existing state of affairs (although an outside enquirer might feel that theirs is the ultimate responsibility) ; they are thus the more ready to admit what is indeed obvious.

The recognition of the retail tailoring trade as an exceptionally bad one, is a growth of the past thirty or forty years. In the days when attention was first drawn to the plight of

workers in the clothing trades, it was commonly the newly-
established wholesale trades that were held up to opprobrium
by comparison with the older and nobler craft of the handicraft
tailor.   This is the attitude displayed in Charles Kingsley's
Alton Locke, and in the same author's *Cheap Clothes and Nasty*.
Not until the Lords' Enquiry of the nineties and the various
Committees and Commissions that succeeded it down to the
time of the passing of the first Trade Boards Act, was it realized
that the journeymen tailors had as much, and in some respects
more, to complain of than their cousins in the factories.   The
campaign against sweating not only opened the eyes of the
public to the nature of these complaints ; it also served as a
reminder to the tailors themselves of the evils with which they
had been so long familiar that they had ceased to regard them
as particularly unusual or as capable of being remedied.   Of
these, the most striking was the enormous part played by
seasonal fluctuations in lowering annual earnings.   Tailors
were now brought face to face with statistical comparisons
between their own and other skilled trades, and, struck by the
difference in income revealed, they naturally determined not
to bring their children up to their own occupation.

It may well be asked why, under these circumstances, the
employers have not endeavoured to ameliorate conditions or
otherwise to induce the rising generation to enter the trade.
The answer is that the normal lines on which new workers in
the handicraft section are trained are such that it has been
nobody's special business to seek them out.   While the
apprentice is not bound to the employer, but to the working
tailor, it is not the latter, but the former, who is likely to
suffer if the labour supply dries up ; and even he will only be
hit by slow degrees and in company with all his fellow employers.   Individual employers have thus neither the incentive
nor the power to act themselves, and, as we have seen, the
working tailors are only too anxious to see their children and

their friends' children escape from an occupation the accompanying evils of which they appreciate from bitter personal experience. The only body which might be expected to make a move is the Association of London Master Tailors. This organization has, it is true, occasionally placed the problem of apprenticeship on its agenda ; but as the only lines along which it could possibly be tackled would involve a vast extension of the indoor system at the expense of the outdoor system of employment, a policy it is not, at the moment anyway, prepared to discuss, no practical proposals for its solution have ever been put forward by the Association.

In the section of the trade represented by the National Federation of Merchant Tailors, doing all but the highest class of bespoke work, the same problem has presented itself. Here the reluctance on the part of parents to bring up their children as tailors was at one time reinforced by a reluctance on the part of many employers to put themselves to the trouble and expense of training young workers. When the influx of trained tailors from the villages began to peter out, they preferred to introduce into their establishments subdivisional methods of work or to resort to the employment of subcontractors, both of which devices enabled them to maintain output with a slowly diminishing force of skilled labour. The inauguration in October 1920 of the first Learners' and Apprentices' rates by the Retail Bespoke Trade Board materially increased this reluctance. The rates were so very much in excess of those which were then current in the trade that objections poured in from all quarters. The employers' contentions were in the main accepted by the workers' representatives, and a new scale was introduced in July 1922. The drop in rates was considerable, as will be seen from the following Table :

REVISED TRADE BOARD RATES—July 1922
General Minimum Time-rate per week of 48 hours

	Males		*Females*	
	New Rates	Old Rates	New Rates	Old Rates
		LEARNERS		
1st year,	9/-	12/-	6/6	10/-
2nd ,,	12/6	15/6	10/-	15/6
3rd ,,	17/6	21/6	16/-	21/6
4th ,,	24/-	30/-	24/-	27/6
5th ,,	34/-	40/-	...	...
		APPRENTICES		
1st year,	7/-	10/-	5/-	8/-
2nd ,,	10/6	12/-	8/-	10/6
3rd ,,	15/-	17/6	12/6	17/6
4th ,,	22/6	25/-	20/-	25/-
5th ,,	32/-	35/-	29/-	34/-

The employers still maintained that the rates were too high. On the other hand, the workers, though they readily admit that it is unreasonable for a learner to expect both a thorough training and a wage approximating to that of a fully qualified worker, complain that in many cases the Learners' rates are regarded by employers as a mere means of getting cheap labour, and that no satisfactory training is provided. In cases where subdivisional methods have been introduced on an extensive scale, there is no doubt good justification for this opinion. However this may be, the N.F.M.T., while still periodically inveighing against the impositions of the Trade Boards, seems now to have made up its mind that Learners' and Apprentices' rates, on a scale sufficient after a short interval to enable the boy or girl to pay for his own keep, have come to stay, and at the same time that employers, if they wish to see a steady flow of new labour into the trade maintained, must devise fresh means of encouraging and training it.

An indication of this new attitude is evidenced by the following extract from an address delivered by the President of the Liverpool branch to the National Society of Tailors' Cutters : " We are faced with a difficult problem of securing youths as apprentices to the bespoke tailoring trade, the chief reason being that the environment of the workshop is far from conducive to the health and well-being of the young man of to-day. Tailors' workshops, especially those where garments are made by hand, have not made an atom of progress during the last forty years." It was partly with the object of securing an influx of learners that the Federation General Workshops Company, alluded to in a previous chapter, was formed. Prominent among the purposes mentioned in its prospectus was that of " training apprentices, assistants, and improvers in the best and most approved tailoring methods as practical tailors." But while co-operative action along these lines is undoubtedly useful, the number of fully-trained tailors it is likely to produce is hardly likely to go very far in meeting the urgent need for them which will probably soon be felt.

Another point that is commonly made when the decay of apprenticeship comes up for discussion is the desirability of improving the facilities at present afforded to boys for learning the art of tailoring before they leave school. In some quarters, in fact, there seems to be a tendency to rely entirely on the establishment of vocational schools as a substitute for the older methods of training. Though much may be done along these lines, it seems certain that such a policy, if pursued in its entirety, would lead to a deterioration in existing standards of skill. What is really wanted, and what has not yet been found, is a means of ensuring to the worker a really thorough training in his craft in return for the acceptance of low pay over a period of several years' apprenticeship. This question of training is the crux of the matter. If it is provided, it is, of course, true that the weekly wage the apprentice

receives is not all he costs his master ; there will be a further
expense due to loss of time by those engaged in teaching him,
and perhaps to spoilt work, etc. It is also true that it will be
worth an apprentice's while to consent to almost any sacrifice
of immediate wages, if in the end he emerges with considerably
enhanced earning powers. On the other hand, it is easy for an
employer to avoid giving value for money, and if this is done,
there is no reason why the young worker should not be paid
at the same rate as his elders, for work of the same quality.

Among the Jewish subdivisional workers the most important
factor in restricting the number of aspirants to the clothing
trades has been the passing of the Aliens' Act of 1911. The
great source of new labour used to be Eastern Europe, whence
young people arrived fully-trained in large numbers every year.
The subcontractor must now turn either to the children of
Jewish workers or else to Gentiles who in the past were scarcely
ever employed in subdivisional workshops. The immigrants
commonly aspired, after a period in the service of a subcontractor, themselves to set up as masters in a small way ;
in fact this was almost invariably the method by which the
Jewish Master Tailors established themselves. The new
recruits are of a less ambitious type, generally seeming content
to learn a single process and remain at it throughout their
working lives. Gradually there seem to be a tendency for the
subdivisional team to grow larger, for handwork to be displaced by machine-work to an even greater degree than in the
past, for the task of each individual to be confined to the
repetition of a single process and so for the system to approxi-
mate to that prevailing in factories. It seems certain that this
tendency will proceed still farther. At the moment the subcontractor is perhaps holding his own in the matter of
numbers, owing to the fact that, while at one end of the scale
he is indistinguishable from the factory owner, at the other he
is displacing the handicraft tailor ; but the ultimate goal

towards which the industry is advancing seems to be one where there will be room only for factories on the one hand and for a very small number of skilled handicraftsmen on the other.

In the factory section of the trade the problems connected with apprenticeship and learnership are naturally less acute. At the same time, there is developing even here a marked shortage of hands with a good all-round training. " In the retail bespoke trade learners are taught all the processes of garment-making, the object being to train them to become *garment* workers, each an independent and complete unit. . . . The advantage to them is very real, but it entails that the learning is more protracted and costly, and that they do not acquire any tangible earning powers for some considerable time after starting as learners. . . . Learners in the wholesale are only taught sectional operations in garment-making, and quickly become competent and develop earning powers. They never become competent to make any garment throughout. They start as sectional workers and remain so, merely becoming cogs in the wheel or interchangeable component parts." The tendency above described is more noticeable in some branches of the wholesale trade than in others. It is least in evidence in the highest class of women's trade ; it is at its worst in the men's clothing factories in Leeds, where the large numbers engaged in the trade permit of a highly specialized labour market. In the smaller centres, such as Bristol, the average worker has a more all-round training ; this is also true in most cases of subdivisional workers employed by Jewish sub-contractors.

For this state of affairs the blame must be attributed partly to the workers and partly to the employers. There is a wide-spread tendency, amongst clothing workers no less than amongst other sections of the adolescent population, to be influenced more by the desire to begin earning good wages as early as possible, than by any anxiety to set out in life with a proper technical equipment. Employers complain that their young workers insist on being put on a piece-rate basis at the earliest possible moment, and that if this request were not acceded to, the workers would at once set about looking for a new situation. They are unwilling to enter into a definite agreement to remain in the employment of the firm which first engages them for a period of years, and in the absence of such an agreement the employer is naturally reluctant to afford them more than the minimum of training. At the same time there is much to be said on the other side. In some branches of the factory trade there has been a marked readiness on the part of unscrupulous employers to take advantage of the Learners' Rates, as laid down by the Trade Boards, to obtain cheap labour. Time and again one comes across cases where girls are engaged at the age of fourteen, and then remain on Learners' Rates for three or four years, only to get taught some special process instead of learning to make a garment throughout. At the end of this period when the law prescribes the payment of a full adult wage, the girls are dismissed and their places taken by younger workers. This abuse is particularly associated with some of the most modern factories, where much of the machinery is semi-automatic, and where, therefore, a worker becomes fully competent to use it after a few hours' or at most a few days' practice. Only when at eighteen she finds herself out of employment does she realize too late that she has been in a blind-alley occupation. Both these questions of vocational training and of blind-alley occupations have long exercised the minds of those interested in the welfare of the rising generation. They will have to be dealt with on national lines, and being in no sense peculiar to the clothing trades, need not detain us further.

CHAPTER IX

THE DECLINE OF HOMEWORK AND SWEATING

IN the foregoing chapters we have endeavoured to present to the reader a picture of the towns where the clothing workers live and work, the trades in which they find employment, the methods by which they are paid and the organizations to which they belong. It remains to attempt a general comparison of the conditions which prevail in the industry to-day, on the one hand, with those which prevailed in it in the past, and, on the other, with those to be found in other industries at the present time. Is it still true to regard the clothing industry as the home *par excellence*, as it has so long been regarded in the past, of the triple evil of long hours, low wages, and insanitary conditions, known as the " sweating system " ; or has this stigma been removed by the improvements which have come about in recent years as the result of the Trade Board Acts and other developments during the past two decades ?

From the sudden awakening in the eighties of the nation's social conscience which led, amongst other events to Charles Booth's enquiry into the life and labour of the London poor, and to the appointment of the House of Lords Committee on sweating, down to the outbreak of the war in 1914, and more particularly during the years which succeeded the *Daily News* " Sweating " Exhibition in 1906, there appeared a very considerable literature, both official and unofficial, dealing with sweated industries in general and the clothing trades in particular. Sensational revelations were not hard to make, and many examples of trouser-finishing, bonnet-making, shirt-making, and indeed all branches of the trade by homeworkers

in East London, at piece-rates which yielded round about
1½d. per hour,[1] may be found in the evidence laid before the
Select Committees on Homework in 1907 and 1908. In such
cases even a sixty or seventy hours' week would fail to yield a
living wage. While it was not suggested in the evidence that
the examples selected as being among the worst were in any
way typical of the trade, it was shown that weekly earnings
below 10s. a week were not uncommon, and that in many cases
these earnings had to support more than one person. In this
latter connection one witness,[2] a Factory Inspector, even
suggested that if a married woman took homework during her
husband's temporary unemployment, she would soon find herself obliged to support the whole family : " Where homework
is increasing, the men show a tendency to rely upon their wives'
labour. . . . I almost agree with the social worker who said
that if the husband got out of work the only thing the wife
should do is to sit down and cry, because if she did anything
else he would remain out of work." It was also shown that the
amount of work to be done was extremely fluctuating, so that
the weekly average wage was not earned throughout the year.
A Board of Trade investigator [3] said, in evidence, that " the
employer aims at keeping his machinery fully employed, and
the factory workers get regular work, because the employer
does not want to waste his machinery ; therefore he will always
give the work to the people in the factory before he gives it to
the homeworkers. That is one of the reasons why the homeworkers' work fluctuates so much." The conditions of work
were in many cases unhealthy : " I frequently find homework
done in one-roomed houses, where the inhabitants live, work
and sleep," said Miss Squire. Miss Vines cited a case in

[1] *E.g.*, Report of Select Committee of 1907, pp. 62, 63 : Evidence of
Miss Vines.

[2] Miss Squire (Factory Inspector). It must, however, be admitted
that other witnesses (*e.g.* Mrs Coppock) disagreed with her on this
point.

[3] Miss Collett.   [4] Select Committee, 1907, p. 63.

London where white silk bonnets were made in a small room in a tenement house inhabited by an old woman and her granddaughters : " The ceiling was absolutely black, the walls were covered with black patches and looked as if they had been scratched all over ; vermin were all over the walls, but the landlord's agent refused to do anything." Conditions in other parts of the country were often as bad, particularly in towns where large numbers of the male population were engaged in casual and especially dock labour, such as Manchester and Glasgow. Miss Irwin,[1] speaking of conditions in Glasgow about the year 1898, informs the Committee that there prevailed " the most objectionable practice of work being used in the dirty homes as bedclothes for sick persons and members of the family generally." In these towns cheap coloured shirts were made at rates which went as low as 10d., or even 6d., a dozen. In certain country districts, especially round Colchester and round Bristol, extremely low earnings were revealed. The following sample from a corset-worker's book was cited in Miss Squire's evidence. The worker was a married woman :

	s.	d.	s.	d.
Making 2 doz. pairs of corsets at 1s. 7½d. a doz.			3	3
Deduct—1½ lb. of cane at 8d. lb. . . .	1	0		
Two reels of cotton at 3d. each . .	0	6		
			1	6
Net wage for 2 dozen pairs . . .			1	9

The worker said it took her three days, working very rapidly, to make the corsets, so that she earned 7d. a day.

Miss Squire added : " I think the corset manufactuıe is one of the worst paid, considering the amount of work to be put into it and the amount of material that the worker has to supply, of any of the clothing trades I know." In Ireland the

[1] Member of Scottish Council for Women's trades. She added that conditions had since improved.
[2] This case occurred in the Bristol district.

wages paid to workers in the villages round Londonderry were exceptionally low, round about 5s. for a full week's work being a common figure. Throughout the south-west of England rates were very low. In the shirt and collar trade round Taunton the practice of giving work to factory workers to do in their own houses after hours was common.[1]

These districts, being the chief centres of homework in the industry,[2] provided most of the more sensational examples. The factory workers in the same districts were generally speaking better off. Under the Factory Acts the premises in which they worked were required to attain certain minimum standards of sanitation and convenience, while hours were limited to $10\frac{1}{2}$ a day. Work, as we have seen, was more regular owing to the employer's reluctance to keep his machinery idle. Wages, even when apparently no higher than those paid for the same class of work done at home, were net wages, whereas the homeworker had to pay for heat, light and any extra accommodation on account of his work which he might be able to afford, as well as in many cases for cotton, etc. Whereas in the factory, machinery was driven by power, at home treadle machines were the general rule. In point of fact, the wages were generally higher in the factories. Miss MacArthur, when questioned by the 1908 Committee on this point, made the following statement : " I should say the wages of manual women workers—if one excepts the skilled trades like the textile trades—rarely reach 7s. a week, taking an average all the year round. (This refers to factory and homework.) Average earnings on homework about 4s. 6d. a week." [3]   In

---

[1] See Miss MacArthur's evidence.

[2] Central London is also an important centre of homework, but will be mentioned later on.

[3] These figures appear at first sight to be unduly low ; but it must be borne in mind that allowance is being made for unemployment and partial employment. They are quoted here for the sake of the comparison, which would be still more striking if the first figure referred *only* to factory work.

regard to hours, Miss Irwin said : " I think homework is accompanied by much longer hours than factory work. The workers work long and irregular hours in their own homes, but they cannot do so in the factories owing to the restrictions of legislation." At the same time, in some of the factories, especially those which employed a good many homeworkers as well, and engaged on a class of trade in which the competition of the homeworker was acute, conditions were far from perfect. Miss MacArthur, after giving evidence about homework, added : " I wish to make clear that the low rates of wages are not confined to homeworkers, and that the question of organization is equally difficult with the similar class of labour in the factory."

In Leeds, the great centre of the better-class ready-made tailoring trade, conditions were much better. Homework in the sense of work done by women working alone in their own homes was comparatively infrequent. Some of the factories employed " outworkers," [1] but these were generally Jewish subcontractors who employed several hands and paid them fairly good wages. Certain other large towns where the clothing trades were solely represented by retail tailors, dressmakers and milliners working for private customers, also presented few serious cases. In Birmingham, for example, where women engaged in the light metal trades were frequently very seriously underpaid, the clothing workers were rather better off. Besides about 1000 factory workers, there were here some 10,000 homeworkers engaged in tailoring, dressmaking and millinery. A careful investigation into the conditions prevailing among homeworkers in Birmingham in 1907, published under the title *Women's Work and Wages* (Cadbury, Matheson and Shann), contains little adverse

---

[1] " Outwork " and " homework " are not synonymous terms. " Outwork " is only " homework " if it is actually done in the home of the worker.

comment on conditions in these trades. The general conclusion of the investigators was that " the evil of sweating in the clothing trades seems to be less prevalent in the Midlands than in London." The wages earned seem to have reached an average of 10s. a week or a little more. In smocking, for instance, which is a fairly large homework industry in the out-skirts of Birmingham, the average was stated to be 10s. or 11s. ; in pinafore-making, 9s. 6d. ; and in tailoring, 11s. 6d. These rates compare very favourably with those earned in such occupations as paper-box-making, leather-work, or burnishing.

Turning to the West End of London we find slightly different problems. The trade here is almost all men's bespoke tailoring, but, as we have seen, it falls into two distinct classes according as the work is done on the one-man-one-garment system, without, or almost without, the use of the machinery ; or on the " sectional " system, where perhaps half a dozen different hands are employed in a " team," each worker specializing on a part of the garment, and where hand-work is used more and more sparingly every year. In the former trade the tailor generally, though not always, employs a woman, paying her from 3s. to 5s. a day to do the less skilled work, such as felling. Coats, waistcoats, and trousers are made by different hands. Before the war as now, pay was nearly always according to the " London log," a peculiarly complicated piece-work scale, nominally on a time basis. Morning-coats worked out from 20s. to 25s., trousers 5s. 9d. to 10s. 6d., overcoats 18s. to 25s. These wages in the busy season might amount to £4 or more a week, but in the slack season they sank to perhaps 30s. The other, and ever-growing section of the trade is almost exclusively Jewish. Only the very highest class of work is now done by the old-fashioned methods ; even in Savile Row it would be hard to find a tailor who has not, in a rush season, had recourse to a high-grade Jewish middleman, employing a team of sectional workers on time-rates. Some of these Jewish workers

M

are male tailors, earning before the war 5s. to 10s. a day ; others, female machinists, earning 15s. to 25s. a week. The reason why the West End trade was often accused of being a " sweated " one was clearly not because the actual rates of pay were unduly low ; the trouble lay with the fluctuating nature of the trade. For two or three months, especially in May and June, work was so plentiful that tailors sometimes found it necessary to remain hard at it all through the night so that a suit ordered for a particular day might be ready in time. The rest of the year, except for a brief revival in December, was comparatively slack, and, in fact, during about five months there was almost nothing to do. Thus rates which were high in themselves reduced themselves to a much lower annual average. Even more serious were the excessive hours during the rush period, especially in view of the insanitary nature of many of the work-places and the rooted objection of the average tailor to any form of ventilation. In the Jewish section of the trade work-places were perhaps healthier, but hours during the season were even longer than among journey-men tailors, since any work which the latter were unable to perform got passed on to the former, who became the shock-absorbers of a fluctuating industry. Mr Daly, Secretary of the West End Branch of the Amalgamated Society of Tailors and Tailoresses, supplied the Homework Committee with information about the effect on the industry of the willingness of the Jewish subcontraction to take on unlimited work, which while clearly animated by an excessively bitter anti-Semitic bias, is borne out by other sources of information.[1] " The Jewish element," he said, " does not make for industrial progress. A young fellow coming over (*i.e.* from the Continent) can be taught almost immediately to become an underpresser.

---

[1] *E.g. Seasonal Trades* (edited by Sidney Webb), 1912, Barbara Drake's section on " Tailoring." But perhaps Mrs Drake obtained much of her information from Mr Daly.

No special skill is required . . . competition as a consequence is rendered very acute, and the result is to bring about a lowering of the standard and a deterioration in the wages and working conditions." He adds : " The trouser section of our industry—the lowest trouser section—is probably the most sweated section in which the lowest prices and the worst conditions obtain." (He is here speaking of domestic workshops and homeworkers ; most of the trouser hands on this class of work were Jews.) And again : " Bad as are the wages paid to Jewish men, those paid by the Jewish masters to English women are even worse." He estimated the average hours among the sectional workers as from 8 A.M. till 9 P.M. (with one hour off for meals), and earnings as about 20s. to 25s. for men and 7s. 6d. to 10s. for women engaged in homework. Another witness [1] said : " The most noticeable feature in recent years is the general adoption of the outworkers' system. I have noticed that in West London in particular workshops are being gradually closed during the last ten or twelve years, and the occupiers are resorting to the outwork practice." Speaking of the long hours he said : " In my night visiting now I very rarely find a place closed. It is quite an exceptional thing to find a place closed even on Sundays, or in the early mornings, such as at 6 A.M. . . . This is particularly so among the homeworkers in Soho." " There is very grave congestion now in London generally, but in Soho in particular. The condition of affairs in Soho is immeasurably worse than it is in East London."

In the course of their report the 1908 Committee summed up the situation in regard to sweating as follows : " If the term ' sweating ' is understood to mean that the employers ' grind the face of the poor ' by making an altogether inadequate payment for work upon which he obtains a large and quite disproportionate profit, your Committee are of opinion that

---

[1] Mr Evans, Factory Inspector's Assistant.

although there are cases of this kind, sweating of this description is not the most important factor in the problem which they have had to consider. On the other hand, if sweating is understood to mean that work is paid for at a rate which in the condition in which many of the workers do it, yields them an income which is quite insufficient to enable an adult person to obtain anything like proper food, clothing and house-accommodation, there is no doubt that sweating does prevail extensively."

If we take 10s. as being the limit below which a weekly wage might be regarded as a " sweated " wage the proportion of sweated women workers *other than homeworkers* in 1906 is revealed by the following Table, extracted from the Board of Trade's " Earnings and Hours of Labour " Enquiry : [1]

Industry	Percentage of Women working Full Time whose Earnings fall within the under-mentioned limits (United Kingdom)		Average Earnings for Full Time.
	Under 10/-	Over 10/-	s. d.
All clothing, including boots and shoes.	21·6	78·4	13 6
Dress, millinery, etc. (factory) .	12·6	87·4	15 5
Tailoring (bespoke) . . .	15·4	86·6	14 2
Dress, millinery, etc. (workshop)	28·0	72·0	13 10
Shirt, blouse, underclothing .	22·2	77·8	13 4
Tailoring (ready-made) . .	24·0	76·0	12 11
Corsets	28·8	71·2	12 2

It must be borne in mind that the above Table probably gives too rosy a picture, since the enquiry was a voluntary one,

[1] See B. L. Hutchins, *Women in Modern Industry*, p. 218.

no employer being compelled to file returns. The absence of uniformity was perhaps more noticeable than the absolutely low level of the average earnings, ordinary wages being as low as 4s. in some cases and as high as 24s. or 25s. in others, though a wage of more than 20s. a week was very rare. The hours worked also showed a fairly wide range of variation. Frequently they were from 8 A.M. till 8 P.M. on ordinary days, and 8 A.M. to 4 P.M. on Saturdays, that is to say, 59 per week (allowing 1½ hours a day for meals). In other cases they were as low as 55 or even 52, but seldom went lower than this.

" Sweating " in the clothing trades is almost confined to women's work. Among the men engaged in the industry the only class whom we might reasonably describe as " sweated " were the London journeymen tailors, and these, as we have seen, rather on account of their long and particularly their irregular hours than because their wages were excessively low. The average earnings of men in factories and workshops, as recorded in the Earnings and Hours Census in 1906, were as follows :

All clothing trades	30/2
Dress, millinery, etc. (workshop) . .	50/11
,, ,, (factory) . . .	31/8
Shirt, blouse, underclothing . . .	29/10
Tailoring (bespoke)	33/6
,, (ready-made)	31/11
Corset (factory)	28/11

(The high average shown for the workshops section of the dress and millinery trade is accounted for by the fact that very few men were here employed. In most cases it is only the more highly-paid work in the clothing trades that is performed by men, though in one section—shirts, blouse, underclothing—as many as 52 per cent. of the male employees were earning less than 30s. a week. But here the numbers employed were also very small.)

The pre-war Trade Boards in the clothing industry were the Shirt Board and the Tailoring Board. The minimum rates fixed by them compare with those given in the 1906 Census as follows :

Trade	Full-time Average Weekly Earnings (1906) Enquiry		Initial T.B. Rates			
			Per hour		Per 50-hr. week	
	Male	Female	Male	Female	Male	Female
Shirt . .	31/1	13/10	– 1	3½	– 1	14/7
Ready-made tailoring .	32/4	12/10	6	3¼	25/-	13/6

It will be seen that in the case of men the Shirt Board did not fix a rate, and the Tailoring Board fixed one lower than the average. But since the average for men includes a substantial proportion of highly-paid workers, it may reasonably be affirmed that the rate fixed was above the minimum previously prevailing rates. The minimum women's rates were above the previous averages, though only slightly so. At the same time it is evident that since the Trade Board rate was a minimum rate, whereas the average quoted covered a wide range, the general level must have been improved considerably except in so far as evasion took place. That evasion did take place on a large scale is certain, and some observers have asserted that among homeworkers the rates have been quite inoperative. While this seems to be an overstatement, there is no doubt that in 1914 there was still much sweating in all branches of the clothing trade where it had existed at the time of the *Daily News* Exhibition.

To what extent can we say that the present state of affairs is an improvement on those which then prevailed ? The most

---

[1] Not fixed, 1914-1919.

noticeable developments affecting the industry since 1914 fall under three heads, namely, fresh legislation, increased organization, and changes in the technique of production. All three have conspired to bring about a situation which on the whole tends to the elimination of the sweated worker. Under the first head the most striking change has been the Trade Boards Act, 1918, which has brought all branches of the industry under the Trade Board system, and has secured for the adult workers in most of them minimum wages of about 7d. per hour (*i.e.* 28s. per week) for women, and 1s. (*i.e.* 48s. per week) for men,[1] in so far as the Act is adequately enforced. It has also tended to make 48 hours the normal week, since overtime rates have to be paid for longer hours.

Cases in which the statutory maximum week for women and children prescribed by the Factory Code is exceeded are accordingly extremely rare, though isolated examples of gross infringement of the law can now and then be discovered. On this point the following extract from the Report of the Chief Inspector of Factories and Workshops for the year 1924 is of interest : " The majority of firms throughout the country have settled down to a normal 47- or 48-hour week. . . . Manufacturers have a very considerable margin of permissible hours left out of the statutory maximum, and accordingly illegal employment is exceptional. . . . (In one case, however), a number of women were employed on mantles and dressmaking from 9 A.M. to midnight for six consecutive days, and also given work to do at home on Sunday. This continued for about a fortnight when, a sufficient stock having accumulated, the workers were dismissed. The women employed showed marked unwillingness to give evidence of illegal employment, and had it not been that they were discharged the offence might never have come to light. The employer was duly convicted and

---

[1] The actual minimum varies slightly in the different sections, and the time-rate is 1d. per hour lower than the piece-rate. The figures quoted are for the lowest-paid adults on time-rates. See also p. 111.

fined £21." It may safely be stated that occurrences of this nature are as unusual as they are distressing.

Another legislative change which was made a little before the war, but the effects of which were only felt after a few years had elapsed, is the Aliens Immigration Restriction Act, 1911. As a result of this law no new recruits have entered the trade from the Continent.[1] This has produced a shortage of labour, and has thus reacted favourably on the earnings and the regularity of employment of the existing workers. Indirectly, too, it has led to the extension of factory work at the expense of the subdivisional system, though for the time being the latter is at least as widespread as ever, owing to the fact that it is itself superseding the handicraft system in the better class trade.

As regards changes in organization the clothing unions shared in the general advance made during the war, particularly in regard to the women workers. There has been a consolidation into two unions (the Amalgamated Society of Tailors and Tailoresses and the United Garment Workers), representing, broadly speaking, the handicraft tailors and the factory workers respectively (apart from some very small Jewish unions and the considerable number of women clothing workers organized in the Shop Assistants' Union and others). As in other trades, the peak reached has not been maintained, a very large proportion of the newly-recruited women having now left the unions, but there has remained a very much stronger basis of organization than in pre-war days. While the unions have thus increased their numbers the employers have also closed their ranks. Before the war there were only a few in any organization at all. Now there are few entirely outside. These associations generally co-operate with the workers'

---

[1] There are at present about 26,000 aliens in the clothing trades, mostly Tailors, Tailors' Pressers and Machinists. Over 80 per cent. of these aliens are Poles or Russians.

unions in securing uniformity of conditions and bringing pressure to bear on backward employers.

Turning to changes in technique, the increased use of power-driven machinery is the most noticeable feature. Much work that fifteen years ago was done by hand or by treadle machine in the workers' homes is now done in factories by power. In the men's trade there has been a very noticeable increase in the wholesale bespoke at the expense of the retail bespoke section, while in the women's trade the mantle and dress factories are driving the small dressmaker out of existence. At the same time in the workshops, power-driven machinery is more and more taking the place of the treadle sewing-machine, especially in the northern towns like Leeds. In fact there has been a minor industrial revolution, so that the industry which before the war was disorganized, and where the typical industrial unit was the small workshop or the solitary homeworker with here and there a large factory, is now comparatively well organized, and usually carried on in a factory or a large workshop, with a small percentage of homeworkers who are tending to disappear still further. One result of these changes has been to diminish very considerably the gravity of the " sweating " problem.

In the early years of the war the cost of living rose more rapidly than did wages, and only in the post-war period can it be said that real wages in the clothing trades were at higher level than before the war. But from the first the numbers of the worst paid section, the homeworkers, declined, owing to the increased opportunities of alternative employment for women, and the smaller volume of unemployment among the husbands of the married women who form a large proportion of the homeworkers. The constant demands of the Government made work, except for high-grade civilian tailors [1] and for dressmakers and milliners, more plentiful, so that both

---

[1] These, however, soon turned to the making of officers' uniforms.

factory workers and homeworkers found themselves in more steady employment.

During 1919 and 1920 all the clothing trades were given Trade Boards, and these Boards proceeded to fix rates of real wages substantially higher than those which had prevailed in 1914. The clothing trades had their share of the post-war prosperity, and wages continued to improve till about the middle of 1921. Then came the slump, with falling wages and widespread unemployment, but without a return to anything like pre-war sweated conditions.

Statistical verification of the diminution in sweating is, of course, impossible to arrive at. All that can be recorded is the impression that was conveyed by conversations in several different centres with representative employers, secretaries of employers' associations, officials of the unions both at the head offices and in the local branches, and by a careful study of the Trade Union publications and of various trade periodicals.

It is true that in the early part of 1924 the *Daily Herald* carried on an anti-sweating campaign ; and there can be no doubt that serious cases could still be found in many parts of the country, and more particularly in the East End and in Soho. It is generally agreed, for instance, that the Trade Board rates are frequently evaded. The question at issue, however, is not whether individual cases still exist, but whether the volume of serious underpayment is as great as before. The opinion of those acquainted with the trade must be our chief guide. The point which emerges most clearly from all inquiries is the diminution in the number of homeworkers.[1] With the single exception of the West End, where the union officials assert that homeworkers form an increasing proportion of the handicraft tailors, there is universal agreement as to this decline. In Leeds, homework is now very rare,

[1] Unfortunately, it is impossible to use the Census to prove this, since an entirely new basis of classification has just been adopted for the occupational tables.

whereas before the war trouser-finishing was given out in fair quantities. In Manchester, where shirts used to be given out, the Secretary of the United Garment Workers says that in face of the smaller demand during the past few years, factories have been unable to keep running full time in any case, and that to give out work would only aggravate the situation.   Even Mr Sullivan, President of the East End Branch of the United Garment Workers, and a witness by no means disinclined to draw a graphic account of the plight of his fellow-workers, agrees that a diminution in the number of homeworkers has taken place.

The principal reason for this decline is undoubtedly the unsatisfactory nature of the work from the employer's point of view. Unless the Trade Board rates are flagrantly disregarded, the employment of homeworkers, except as a means of tiding over a " rush " period with which the existing factory accommodation is unable to cope, has become an unremunerative practice. Apart from the question of rates, the legal requirements in regard to registration of premises, etc., are a source of considerable worry, which is saved by having all work done inside the factory. To this may be added the recent developments in the sewing-machine industry which have made it possible to perform mechanically even such operations as were till very recently done by hand, e.g. button-holing. In one section where homework and sweating used to be common, namely, underwear, a change in the type of garment worn has had a considerable effect. Here the newly developed woven underwear trade is rapidly driving flannel and calico out of existence as materials for underwear. The woven garments are made by machinery throughout, requiring either no sewing at all or a negligible amount of sewing. In the old days it was stated that if the cheaper grades of underwear were to find a market at all it was necessary to sell them at so low a figure that sweated labour was almost inevitable ; otherwise the clothes would be made at home. Nowadays, the number of women who either have time or inclination to make their clothes at home has considerably diminished, and the cheapness of the factory-made woven garments has led to their general adoption even among the poorer classes of the community. In this connection, too, may be mentioned the vast increase which has recently been taking place in the factory section of the mantle and dressmakers' trade. Changing fashions have lessened the demand for tailor-made coats and skirts. The type of dress usually worn to-day can be made, and is almost invariably made, by very much the same methods as the cheaper grades of men's clothing—in large factories in Leeds and Manchester, and elsewhere. The private dressmakers are going out of business, and with them has gone another section of the trade in which conditions were apt to be bad. For instance, it used to be not uncommon for girls to be taken on for two or three years by dressmakers without earning any wages at all, on the plea that they were " learning the trade." The dressmakers who still survive are constantly complaining that the learners' rates fixed by the Trade Boards are unduly high. What they mean is that just as it used to be necessary to pay unduly low wages in order to sell at prices which would prevent clothes being made at home, so now it is necessary to do the same in order to sell at prices which will compete with those charged for factory-made ready-to-wear articles. A final reason for the decline in the amount of homework is the slump in trade. As has been indicated above, in the case of the Manchester shirt-trade, there is at the present moment more factory accommodation in most branches of the clothing trade than there is any need for. If and when the demand for clothes increases to such an extent that the factories are unable to cope with it, we may see a revival of homework, especially in the " finishing " of men's suits. Such a revival, however, is likely to be temporary and, in any case, with the gradual tightening up of Government inspection, is unlikely to be accompanied by exceptionally low rates of pay. The foregoing conclusions, which are reproduced from an article by the present writer in *Economica* (March 1927), were arrived at independently. It is interesting to note that they are borne out by the following extract from the Report of the Chief Inspector of Factories and Workshops for the year 1925 :

" A special enquiry has been carried out with a view to ascertaining the present position regarding homework, and reports have been submitted by the Women Deputy Superintending Inspectors for each Division.

"*Industries in which Homework Prevails.*—Homework prevails in a great variety of trades, and is found, as Miss Anderson points out, in (*a*) old-established industries carried on in rural districts by genuine home-workers, *e.g.* lace-making, glove-making ; in (*b*) well-established factory industries carried on in industrial areas, *e.g.* tailoring ; in (*c*) temporary industries arising out of a fashion demand, which consequently can be more conveniently met by the employment of additional labour in the form of homeworkers than by obtaining larger premises, *e.g.* ladies' hair ornaments, which have now died out owing to the fashion for shingled hair ; and in (*d*) purely local industries, *e.g.* pea-picking in Boston, shrimp-picking in Morecambe.

" Generally, however, the industries in which homework is found may be classified under such headings as ' Wearing Apparel,' ' Food Trades,' ' Metal Industries,' and ' Miscellaneous Trades.'

"Under the heading of ' Wearing Apparel,' we have tailoring, dressmaking, embroidery, boot- and shoe-making and repairing, lace, hosiery, hats, caps, gloves, swansdown trimming, underclothing, shirts, collars, umbrellas, handkerchiefs, weaving and mending tweed, textile smallwares, corsets, children's frocks, bishops' aprons and widows' caps. . . . (Here follows a list of the homework trades comprised under the headings ' Food Trades,' ' Metal Industries,' and ' Miscellaneous Trades.')

" *General Character of the Work*.—The trades in which homework is to be found are so many and varied that the general character of the work given out is also multifarious. Although a considerable amount of it is unskilled, as, for example, the putting of strings into labels, and is of such a type as not to require much supervision, there is a great deal which is highly skilled and of a specialized nature. High-class tailoring and boot- and shoe-making come under this latter heading, and it is found in many cases that this class of work is given out to employees who have married and left the factory, but whose work and skill can be relied on. Between these extremes there is a fair amount of work which must be regarded as semi-skilled and for which outworkers are not trained by the firms, but ' teach each other.'

" Homework is generally handwork, and the tools required can be obtained with small outlay, except in the case of weaving on a hand-loom or machining on a treadle sewing-machine, and much of it depends on the use of a needle or paste-brush. Often the work is cut out or prepared before it is sent to the homeworker.

" But the use of electricity is bringing mechanical power even into the homes of the outworker, and Miss Dingle in the course of her visits in the Eastern Counties found several electrically-driven machines in the workers' living rooms. She found, for example, a hosiery-linking machine (with low shafting not securely fenced), three boot-closing machines, and two straw-hat machines, all driven by electric motors. This is a comparatively new departure, and cheaper electricity and its more universal use will probably bring about an increase in the number of such machines.

" Homework is, of course, piece-work, and although no

specific enquiry was made, except in the trades governed by legal enactments,[1] it appeared that the workers were usually aware of the price they were to receive for their work.

"*Reasons for Outwork.*—The reasons given by occupiers for employing outworkers rather than having their work done in their own premises and under their own observation are many and various. In addition to the obvious reasons that this form of work lessens the cost of production by saving overhead charges, and reducing the amount which has to be spent on rent and unemployment insurance, and transfers to someone else the duty of complying with legal requirements, there are many others which have a direct bearing on the matter. Some of the industries in which work is given out are so old that the present employers have had no part in the establishment of the system, and have taken it over as they found it. Many of the outworkers are women who at one time, probably previous to their marriage, worked inside the factory, where they became skilled. Their employment as outworkers after marriage enabled the occupier to retain the advantage of their skill and enabled them to continue their work, which would have been impossible if it had to be carried on for regular and specified periods in a factory. Especially is this the case where they live scattered about the countryside in places which suit their husbands' work, but which are too far away from centres to make daily journeys possible. Then the very fact that much of the outwork is intermittent makes the system valuable to the employer, as in times of emergency he can fall back on these outdoor workers. If they are not entirely dependent on the work, the employer feels no responsibility for them when the work is short, and also he is not compelled to obtain extension of premises for seasonal trade. On the other hand, some employers continue to employ outworkers for what may

[1] This includes the clothing trades, together with all the other industries subject to the Trade Board regulations.—S. P. D.

be termed sentimental reasons, realizing that the additional income will be of great assistance.

" Another important reason for employing them is that in some leases a clause is inserted forbidding manufacture on the premises, while in other cases the rents in streets with a high reputation as shopping centres are so heavy that firms find they cannot afford to maintain workrooms on the premises.

" There is much to be said, too, in favour of homework from the point of view of the individual worker. Undoubtedly, many women welcome the opportunity of being able to continue their work after marriage, and if they have young children or invalid relatives depending on their attention, they cannot leave them, but they can spend any spare time they may have in homework, and so add to the family means.

" *Compliance with Act.*—Considerable enquiry was made into how far there was compliance with the requirements of sect. 107 of the Act in connection with the keeping of lists of outworkers and the forwarding of them twice yearly to the Local Authority. It was found that generally speaking the standard of compliance with this requirement was high, particularly in the boroughs and urban districts. This was probably due to the fact that this section is enforced by the Factory Inspectors at their visits and by the officers of the Local Authority, who remind firms of their obligations. Indeed, it is a regular practice with some authorities to send out reminders systematically. In one city, for example, about 600 notices are annually served on occupiers reminding them of their duty in this respect ; other cities have their own reprint of Form 44, which they send out twice yearly with a covering letter to all occupiers known to be employing outworkers ; while in yet another the Sanitary Inspectors take round forms and assist the smaller or employers of foreign extraction to fill them up. On the other hand, in the case of areas under some authorities, few returns are sent in, and these are in many cases inaccurate. Miss Sadler reports ' that certain Medical Officers of Health have expressed grave doubts as to the accuracy of the lists, and suggest that they are not complete records of all the officers employed, and that a firm does not always care to give the name and address of a skilled homeworker. Also that a firm which pays low wages does not want to risk the chance of being shown up. More than one official in charge of the lists has suggested that the occupiers only send in the names of the workers actually employed at the time that the list is sent in ; other homeworkers employed during the intervening months may escape record.' Undoubtedly the observance of the requirement depends largely on the vigilance of the Local Authority.

" The notification of outworkers' homes is followed up in some towns by systematic visiting on the part of special officers appointed for the purpose, with satisfactory results. In other towns, the Health Visitors and Sanitary Inspectors only make such inspections in connection with their other work, *e.g.* maternity and child-welfare or ' house-to-house ' inspection, and in these places little value is attached to obtaining the lists.

" Although there appears to be fair compliance with the requirement that lists of outworkers must be kept in the factory or workshop, Miss Meiklejohn has found in Scotland that in many cases the list is not ' kept,' but prepared only for the purpose of being forwarded to the Sanitary Authority. This practice overlooks the fact that the section requires that a list shall be kept continuously in the factory, and that twice yearly copies of these lists shall be sent to the District Council.

" *Increase or Decrease in Outworkers.*—Examination of the lists of outworkers and enquiry from Local Authorities have made it clear that there is a decrease in the number of homeworkers employed since the war. For various reasons the figures obtainable cannot be taken as giving the exact number

N

of homeworkers. For example, the lists are in most cases received twice a year, so that about double the number of outworkers would be shown, but in other cases they have been forwarded once only. Then again, outworkers are employed by more than one firm and will appear on more than one list. It was also suggested in one town that the prescribed periods for return coincide with periods of slack trade when reduced staffs are employed. On the other hand, it was found that workers are kept on the lists who have very intermittent, if any, employment throughout the year. In order to ensure that exact particulars of the number of outworkers are available, more careful scrutiny of the lists would be necessary than is usually the case. Even, however, without such scrutiny, there is a consensus of opinion that homework is on the decline, *except in the tailoring trade, where outwork (not necessarily homework) is still common*,[1] and in certain trades related to household furnishing and equipment, where there is a slight increase, due possibly to temporary causes, such as the demand for the new homes which have been established. Indeed, those engaged in some trades suggest that homework will be limited to the lives of the present homeworkers.

" There appear to be certain general reasons which are causing this decrease. For example, it is impossible, as Miss Taylor reports, to dissociate it from the general decline in trade ; outworkers are frequently only part-time workers, and they tend to be the first whose services are dispensed with when work is short. Then again, as the same Inspector points out, ' outworkers are casual workers and there is not much room for casual work in modern industry, and outwork has not in the past, with few exceptions, been well organized, and it has been difficult to secure that the work was properly done and delivered at the moment that it was wanted. Formerly these disadvantages were probably counteracted to a certain extent

---

[1] Italics mine.—S. P. D.

by the fact that the labour though casual was cheap. The development of Trade Boards has removed that advantage.' Other reasons for decrease in homework are the invention of new machinery, the cheapening of power, and the extension of the use of electricity—closely connected with which is the growth of the practice of subdivision of labour—and the provision of more commodious and up-to-date factory premises. Occupiers with sufficient accommodation do not wish to go to the trouble and expense of checking work in and out of the factory nor to submit to the delay which often arises in connection with outwork ; and further, in some districts the improvement in means of locomotion which allows workers to travel daily to industrial centres from the surrounding country villages has resulted in less homework being given out. Undoubtedly also to the younger worker homework is not attractive. They complain that it is monotonous and does not enable them ' to see life.'

" Generally speaking, outwork appears to be considerably influenced by tradition, and there is no evidence that many new processes are being given to homeworkers.

" *Working Conditions.*—As one of the main reasons for legislation in connection with homework was to ensure that work should not be carried on in unwholesome premises, special enquiry was made into the prevalence of the employment of persons in such premises.

" It was satisfactory to find that there was little evidence of work being carried on in ' unwholesome premises ' within the meaning of sect. 108, *i.e.* so serious as to require stoppage of work. There were, however, of course, many cases in which sanitary defects of various degrees of severity, especially in regard to cleansing and lime-washing, had been dealt with from time to time. Miss Kelly found in the course of her visits some bad conditions, such as leaking roofs and defective flooring caused by rats. These were referred to the Local

Authority, which was found to be already dealing with them. On the whole, however, there is evidence to show that the persons taking outwork are not generally those living in dirty houses ; instead, they are of a better class and their homes are usually clean. Miss Taylor considers that the diminution in numbers of outworkers has had a good effect on the quality of the premises. It has been possible to retain the more desirable outworkers on the lists and to get rid of those whose houses were unsuitable. She has also found that much good work is done by the Sanitary Inspectors by way of warning to the women, and, if necessary, complaint to the employer in cases in which the houses are not too clean, and the threat of withdrawal of work generally has the desired effect.

" Similar conclusions have been interestingly summarized by Miss Anderson as follows :

" In two cities systematic inspection of outworkers' premises and homes is carried on by a staff appointed for the purpose, and the Chief Sanitary Inspector of one of them reported that far from being carried on in the poorer types of dwelling, outwork was taken in to supplement their resources by many people whose names one would never expect to find on an outworkers' list, and that he only wished that some of the poorer types would take in homework, as it would indicate some desire on their part to improve their circumstances and give him an opportunity of trying to improve the sanitary condition of their dwellings by the inspection and advice of his women Inspectors. . . .

" Although outwork is common in many trades, the fact remains that tailoring is the principal industry in which outworkers are employed. It is therefore of interest, in conclusion, to deal with this trade in some detail. The workers, far from being casual, are in most instances entirely dependent on the work sent out by the factories. Accurate information as to the numbers employed is difficult to obtain, as the figures

are usually included under wearing apparel, but evidence
points to the fact that although there has been no sudden
increase, there has been no decrease but a comparative steadi-
ness in the numbers.   It is becoming more and more the
custom for retail bespoke tailors only to cut and fit and to send
out the actual making to these factories and workshops, or to
skilled workers who work at home or rent benches in tenement
premises.   There are various reasons for this development.
The shop or showroom premises must be within the shopping
area of the town, and the rents in these areas are now so prohibitive that it is impossible to have large workrooms on the
same site.   In one large city, Mr Duffield reports that it is
customary to find a tailor occupying a small office with a
cutting and fitting room in most blocks of office premises
adjoining the markets and exchanges.   The tailor is on the
spot for his clientele, but as the rents of such neighbourhoods
are prohibitively high for a workshop, he gives out the actual
making.   Further, the bespoke trade is largely seasonal.   If
an occupier has a dozen skilled men on his indoor staff, he
will at intervals have little work for them.   If he employs
them as outworkers, he incurs no responsibility and no expense
with regard to them during the slack time.

" In the smaller towns, homework in the tailoring trade seems
to be declining and the custom of giving outwork to small
factories and workshops is rare.   Factory-made garments now
compete seriously with bespoke work, and the establishment of
branches of multiple shops takes a great deal of trade away
from local firms.   Measurements are taken at these shops and
sent to the factories where the orders are executed.   These
factories have adopted extensively the system of sectionalizing
the work, which, as far as possible, is done by machinery.

" The wholesale or ready-made trade is largely done for export, and many of the firms employ contractors who work for
them in the busy seasons in their own workshops.   Homework

has not increased in this branch of the trade. Miss Ahrons, who reports at length on the tailoring trade as carried on in Leeds, is of the opinion that there is no evidence that homework has increased in the trade as a whole. She considers that any increase there is would be found in the high-class retail section, especially in London and other large cities. The growth of multiple shops and the practice of making all garments off the premises may have led to a conclusion that homework has increased. This view is erroneous ; what has occurred is that the work is being done in large factories."

As regards the work done in factories and workshops, conditions may be said to be fairly good. As in other industries, 48 hours has become the normal week, and the Trade Boards have adopted this as the standard beyond which overtime rates must be paid. It is agreed by the union officials that Trade Board rates are nearly always observed,[1] and in many cases considerably higher rates are paid. One abuse, however, still seems to be pretty general, and that is the failure to pay for " waiting " time. The law requires that where a worker is kept on the employer's premises waiting for work, he shall be paid as if he were actually working. This is frequently not done, and owing to the strong temptation which the worker feels to connive at the infringement, it is difficult to see how this can be remedied. Another practice, which amounts to preserving the letter of the law, while infringing the spirit, is the employment by some firms of juvenile workers at learners' rates, when they are in effect doing an ordinary adult worker's work. A firm in Manchester, one of the largest in the knitted

---

[1] The officials often speak of these wages as being shamefully low, *e.g.*: At a meeting of the Tailors' and Garment Workers' Union on 10th June, 1924, Mr. Conley, Secretary, said a fight would be made to secure a minimum wage of £4 a week for males and £3 for females, together with a 44-hour week. A comparison of these figures with the actual rates being paid, even to skilled workers in other trades, will show that they are quite Utopian. Mr. Conley does not indicate whether he is referring to skilled workers only, or to all workers.

underwear trade in the country, is alleged by the union officials to employ a staff which consists almost exclusively of girls under 18. The machines employed are almost self-acting, so that a few days suffices to learn the process. The girls are engaged at 14 or 15, and on reaching the age of 18, when full-time adult rates have to be paid, are dismissed and replaced by a fresh batch.

Sanitary conditions in factories vary considerably from firm to firm. Where the factory has been specially built for use as a clothing factory there is usually adequate space and light. In many cases, however, the factories have only been adapted for the purpose. This is true of all the centres of the industry, including Leeds. In these makeshift factories the light which is so essential for a sewing industry is obscured by large adjacent buildings. Frequently also the piles of material stacked in the workrooms are so large as to prevent the legal minimum of air space per worker being reached. Generally speaking, however, it may be said that in the factories of the present day, as also in the workrooms of the big department stores (by many of which special agreements with the workers have been made), conditions reach a satisfactory standard.

It is when we come to the workshop section of the trade that conditions generally leave most to be desired. It is not that wages are specially low ; on the contrary, they sometimes reach an exceptionally high level. In London, for instance, 10d. per hour for women and 14s. a day for men are practically minima. There is a distinct shortage of labour, particularly of male labour. The workers are nearly always Jews, though gradually it is being found necessary to take on Christians. In the past the workers arrived in this country from the Continent ready trained, but since the passing of the Aliens Immigration Act in 1911 there has been no influx of foreign labour. The children of the Jews who have settled do not usually enter the trade, and skilled workers are thus becoming more and more difficult to obtain. While there is this shortage of labour there is also an increasing demand for clothes made on the subdivisional system, partly owing to the high cost of handicraft tailoring and partly to the even more acute shortage of labour in the handicraft section. This state of affairs ensures a high level of wages. But while the pay is good the conditions are frequently bad, especially in London. Even Mr Marks, of the Master Tailors' Association, admits [1] that it is an unpleasant " trade," and that it is hard for this reason to find new recruits. There are still, in London, hundreds of workshops in which perhaps six to ten workers are cramped into a small room, with poor ventilation, an atmosphere made damp by the pressing which is frequently performed in the same room as the sewing and machining, and where Government inspection is unknown.

Among the handicraft workers conditions have also not improved. In fact, since the tendency is now for less and less work to be done on the employer's premises, and more and more at the worker's home or in hired " sittings," they are perhaps worse. We have already seen, however, that the handicraft worker is giving way to the subdivisional worker, and he in turn to the factory operative. It is this displacement which enables the comparison between the lot of the typical pre-war worker and the typical post-war worker to be regarded as definitely favourable to the latter.

Finally, a comparative consideration of conditions in other industries amply justifies the belief that the clothing trade has mounted the industrial ladder. It has shared the lot of the other sheltered industries, catering as it does almost entirely for a home market. In particular it has shared the lot of the other Trade Board trades in which wages were fixed at a high level in 1921, and where the stickiness of the Trade Board

[1] " Master Tailor " is the name given to themselves by the Jewish subcontractors.

system has impeded a reduction to the level which would undoubtedly have been reached under conditions of free competition. It has also fared better than other industries in regard to unemployment during the recent slump. Seasonal it still is, but less seasonal than before, since factories can make for stock. Apart from seasonal variation the demand for clothing is less elastic than for many other things. The necessity for buying new clothes may be temporarily averted by wearing out old ones, but ultimately nearly as many as usual must be bought by the vast majority of mankind, while in the case of the more well-to-do classes who buy more clothes than they need, economy in luxuries is more likely to begin with travelling or books or furniture than with clothes, which are to some extent to be regarded as " conventional necessities " (by the economist as well as by the student of manners !). An examination of the monthly unemployment returns— published in the *Ministry of Labour Gazette*—will show that this inelasticity of demand has conspired with the reduced supply of workers to place clothing low down on the list of unemployment percentages. With shorter hours, higher real wages, and better conditions than before the war, and with less unemployment than many other workers, the clothing operative can no longer be regarded as the Cinderella of modern industry.

BIBLIOGRAPHY

NOTE.—The following bibliography makes no attempt to be exhaustive, but merely indicates some of the principal sources of information, other than personal enquiry, on which the foregoing chapters are based. It will be seen that the great bulk of them are official Government publications or the journals and periodicals of trade unions and employers' organizations.

A. *Government Publications* :

Census of Production, 1907. Final Report, 1912–13. [Cd. 6320.]
Board of Trade Enquiry into Earnings and Hours. Part II. Clothing Trades in 1906. (1909.) [Cd. 4844.]
Report from Select Committee on Homework, 1907–1908.
Report on the Administration of the Factory and Workshop Act, 1901, in respect of Outwork, etc., in 1907 (1909). [Cd. 4633.]
Report of War Cabinet Committee on Women in Industry (1919). [Cmd. 135.]
Report of Committee appointed to enquire into the Working and Effects of the Trade Boards Acts. (1902.) [Cmd. 1645.] (The Cave Committee.)
Statement of Government's Policy in regard to Trade Boards Acts pending legislation. (1922.) [Cmd. 1712.]
Annual Reports of the Chief Inspector of Factories and Workshops.
Annual Reports of the Ministry of Health.
Annual Reports of the Ministry of Labour.
Ministry of Labour Gazette.
1921 Census of Great Britain.

B. *Other Publications :*

BLACK, CLEMENTINA. *Sweated Industry and the Minimum Wage.* Duckworth & Co. London, 1907.
BLACK, CLEMENTINA and MEYER (Mrs. A.). *Makers of our Clothes.* Duckworth & Co. London, 1909.

BOOTH, Rt. Hon. CHARLES. *Life and Labour of the People in London.* Macmillan & Co. London, 1902, 1903. See especially Vol. IV. c. III., "The Tailoring Trade," by Beatrice Potter; c. V. Section (2) "West End Tailoring (Men)," by James Macdonald; and Section (3) "West End Tailoring (Women)," by Clara E. Collet.

BOWLEY, A. L. *Prices and Earnings in Time of War.* Oxford Pamphlets. 1915.

BOWLEY, A. L. *Prices and Wages in the United Kingdom.* 1914–1920. Oxford, 1921. (Economic and Social History of the World War. British Series.)

BURNS, E. M. *Wages and the State.* P. S. King & Son, 1926.

CADBURY, MATHESON and SHANN. *Women's Work and Wages.* T. Fisher Unwin, 1907.

DRAKE, BARBARA. *Women in Trade Unions.* Labour Research Department. London (1921). (Trade Union Series. No. 6.)

GALTON, F. W. *The Tailoring Trade. Select Documents illustrating Trade Unionism.* Longmans, Green & Co., 1896.

HUTCHINS, B. L. *Women in Modern Industry.* G. Bell & Sons. London, 1915.

HUTCHINS, B. L. *The Present Position of Industrial Women Workers.* Macmillan & Co. London, 1921.

HUTCHINS, B. L. and SPENCER, A. *History of Factory Legislation.* Third edition. P. S. King & Son. London, 1926. (London School of Economics. Studies in Economics and Political Science. No. 10.)

SELLS, DOROTHY. *The British Trade Boards System.* P. S. King & Son. London, 1923. (Studies in Economic and Political Science. No. 70.)

TAWNEY, R. H. *Poverty as an Industrial Problem.* London School of Economics. Ratan Tata Foundation. 1913. Memoranda on Problems of Poverty. No. 2.

TAWNEY, R. H. *The Establishment of Minimum Rates in the Tailoring Industry under the Trade Boards Act of* 1909. London School of Economics. Ratan Tata Foundation. Studies in the Minimum Wage.

WEBB, SIDNEY and BEATRICE. *The History of Trade Unionism.* Revised edition extended to 1920. Longmans & Co. London, 1920.

WEBB, SIDNEY and BEATRICE. *Industrial Democracy.* Longmans & Co. London, 1920.

WEBB and FREEMAN (ed.). *Seasonal Trades' Section on*

Tailoring. C. II., "The Tailoring Trade," by Barbara Drake. Constable & Co., 1912.

National Union of Women Workers, Handbook and Report, 1910, etc.

Reports of the National Anti-Sweating League.

The Merchant Tailor. (Monthly organ of the National Federation of Merchant Tailors.)

The Sartorial Gazette.

Journal of the Amalgamated Society of Tailors and Tailoresses. (Manchester ; quarterly.)

The Garment Worker. (Monthly organ of the Tailors' and Garment Workers' Trade Union. Leeds.)

International Labour Review, Vol. XVIII, Nos. 1 and 2 (July and August 1928). Articles on "Seasonal Unemployment in the Clothing Trades." (International Labour Office.)

APPENDIXES

APPENDIX I.—NUMBERS ENGAGED IN THE CLOTHING TRADES

(a) ENGLAND AND WALES

Persons engaged in the principal sections of the clothing trades in England and Wales, and in certain industrial districts, as follows:

District I.—Greater London.

,,   II.—Lancashire and parts of Cheshire and Derbyshire.

,,   III.—Yorkshire, West Riding and City of York.

,,   IV.—North-east Coast.

,,   V.—Birmingham District (including Birmingham, Coventry, Dudley, Bromsgrove, Walsall, Wolverhampton, etc.)

,,   VI.—South Wales.

		England and Wales	I	II	III	IV	V	VI
Tailoring (including Mantles)	M	126,451	43,844	18,210	15,734	2,979	4,255	2,656
	F	161,749	41,601	29,677	30,855	4,444	6,911	3,009
Dress and Blouse	M	4,115	2,366	406	227	29	51	26
	F	146,330	49,781	15,834	8,861	4,491	4,592	5,823
Shirts, Collars and Overalls	M	4,449	1,940	857	181	32	93	19
	F	27,331	9,142	5,248	1,949	279	1,838	149
Stays and Corsets	M	2,083	444	141	25	3	23	5
	F	12,636	1,894	1,109	180	44	231	34
Underclothing	M	1,323	589	354	91	16	26	3
	F	11,204	4,247	4,243	899	173	406	3
Handkerchiefs, Scarves and Ties	M	800	608	87	5	...	1	...
	F	2,895	2,108	440	7	...	2	1
Millinery	M	2,399	1,441	277	89	18	34	14
	F	38,092	13,701	6,713	2,962	1,568	2,010	1,040
Total of above	M	141,620	51,232	20,332	16,352	3,077	4,483	2,723
	F	400,217	122,474	63,264	45,113	10,999	15,990	10,059

Note in the foregoing Table the enormous preponderance of Districts I, II, and III, *i.e.* London, Lancashire and the West Riding, which between them comprise 318,767 out of the 541,837 workers enumerated. London, in particular, has over one-third of the total males and not far short of one-third of the total females enumerated.

(b) SCOTLAND

Persons engaged in the principal sections of the clothing trades in Scotland and in certain cities :

		Scotland	Edinburgh	Glasgow	Dundee	Aberdeen
Tailoring (includ-	M	14,102	1,508	3,994	426	643
ing Mantles)	F	15,613	1,508	7,482	340	571
Dress and Blouse	M	224	25	121	3	6
	F	14,850	1,489	3,728	366	582
Shirts, Collars and	M	415	14	240	5	...
Overalls	F	2,919	54	1,996	8	15
Stays and Corsets	M	27	5	10	...	...
	F	283	24	153	6	9
Underclothing	M	95	3	60	2	1
	F	925	8	686	25	17
Handkerchiefs,	M	37	2	25	...	...
Scarves and Ties	F	214	2	176	...	...
Millinery	M	76	11	41	...	6
	F	2,511	284	607	119	162
Total of above	M	14,976	1,568	4,491	436	650
	F	37,315	3,369	14,828	864	1,356

Note the preponderance of Glasgow—19,319 out of a total of 52,291, *i.e.* well over one-third. This proportion would be considerably increased by including the surrounding industrial district.

(c) CLOTHING TRADES

ENGLAND AND WALES

Comparative Table of numbers engaged in 1901, 1911 and 1921 (in thousands) :

		1901	1911(1)[1]	1911(2)[1]	1921
All clothing (*i.e.* including boots and shoes, etc.)	Males	338	333	346	312
	Females	687	711	703	503
	Total	1025	1044	1050	815
Tailoring	Males	120	123	131	126
	Females	118	127	131	162
	Total	237	250	262	288
Dressmaking	Males	1	4	6	7
	Females	389	406	395	184
	Total	391 [2]	410 [2]	401 [2]	191 [2]
Hats and Caps	Males	16	18	19	15
	Females	23	22	23	20
	Total	39	40	43	35
Boots, Shoes and Clogs	Males	184	169	172	146
	Females	45	45	46	52
	Total	229	214	218	198

[1] Comparison between 1921 and 1911 is affected by changes in the methods of classification ; the figures for 1911(2) are adjusted so as to be comparable with those for 1921.

[2] Note the enormous drop in this section in the period 1911-1921.

APPENDIX II.—EARNINGS

The following Table of average weekly earnings is taken from the Ministry of Labour *Gazette* (November 1926). The Table shows the average actual earnings per head, in the four specified weeks of 1924 of the work-people employed by the firms making returns, together with the average earnings of males and of females, as shown by those returns which gave separate particulars. It should be observed that the work-people covered by the returns include workers of all ages, including boys and apprentices and other juveniles.

The relative levels of average earnings shown for the different industries are, of course, affected by the variations in the proportions of adults and juveniles employed.

Industry	Number of Work-people Covered	Average Earnings (for time actually worked) in the week ended				Average of the Earnings in the four weeks
		19th Jan. 1924	12th April 1924	12th July 1924	18th Oct. 1924	
(A) MALES						
		s. d.	s. d.	s. d.	s. d.	s. d.
Tailoring (retail bespoke) .	6,706	49 2	60 7	57 6	55 9	55 11
Tailoring (ready-made) .	15,436	53 1	61 10	59 6	57 2	58 0
Dressmaking . . .	746	50 4	52 11	52 3	53 6	52 3
Mantle- and costume-making	2,095	63 2	68 5	64 8	67 3	65 11
Shirt, blouse, etc., making .	2,962	53 5	54 1	54 3	53 6	53 10
Corset-making . . .	340	51 5	52 10	51 11	49 10	51 6
Millinery	646	44 2	47 3	44 2	44 0	44 11
Felt- and silk-hat-making .	2,849	52 3	58 2	62 11	57 10	57 11
Boot- and shoe-making (be-spoke) and repairing .	12,222	49 6	50 9	51 11	51 6	50 11
Boot- and shoe-making (ready-made) . . .	43,425	53 9	56 3	55 8	53 9	54 11
Glove-making . . .	2,023	49 9	55 3	58 7	55 8	54 10
Furriery	2,349	61 7	66 2	62 10	66 2	64 3
Laundries . . .	10,012	48 3	48 3	48 2	48 0	48 2
Dyeing and dry-cleaning .	2,474	53 10	55 6	55 0	54 2	54 8
Other clothing . . .	9,471	53 4	57 0	57 0	57 4	56 3
All the above . .	113,756	52 7	56 5	55 9	54 6	54 10
(B) FEMALES						
		s. d.	s. d.	s. d.	s. d.	s. d.
Tailoring (retail bespoke) .	8,197	25 2	30 0	29 6	27 5	28 2
Tailoring (ready-made) .	43,824	24 10	28 5	27 1	25 11	26 7
Dressmaking . . .	30,130	27 2	28 6	29 0	28 6	28 4
Mantle- and costume-making	11,849	28 5	30 10	29 8	29 8	29 8
Shirt, blouse, etc., making .	38,516	24 7	25 9	25 7	24 9	25 2
Corset-making . . .	3,250	22 7	25 2	24 4	22 7	23 8
Millinery . . , .	11,867	28 7	28 7	27 11	26 11	28 0
Felt- and silk-hat-making .	2,628	23 9	27 6	25 9	25 7	25 8
Boot- and shoe-making (be-spoke) and repairing .	1,409	26 11	27 7	27 2	27 11	27 5
Boot- and shoe-making (ready-made) . . .	28,534	30 7	31 1	31 7	30 1	30 10
Glove-making . . .	3,047	19 8	21 5	22 11	23 0	21 9
Furriery	2,830	33 11	36 8	38 0	40 4	37 3
Laundries . . .	53,692	26 10	26 9	26 10	26 2	26 8
Dyeing and dry-cleaning .	4,445	25 0	28 8	27 10	28 8	27 7
Other clothing . . .	39,405	26 3	28 5	27 5	27 0	27 3
All the above . .	283,623	26 6	28 2	27 9	27 0	27 5

APPENDIX III.—METHODS OF WAGE-PAYMENT IN THE CLOTHING TRADES.

A. Tailoring.

(1) *Retail Bespoke :*

    (*a*) Log-rates.

    (*b*) Piece-rates for each separate process (very similar to log-rates).

    (*c*) Piece-rates per garment to each worker engaged on it. In a few cases country tailors pay their men a single piece-rate for the entire garment.

    (*d*) Time-rates. Only common in the shops of Jewish subcontractors and the tailoring departments of large stores.

(2) *Wholesale Bespoke and Ready-made :*

    (*a*) Piece-rates (normally) to tailors and tailoresses, machinists, buttoners, button-holers, embroidery machinists, etc.

    (*b*) Time-rates (normally) to foremen, checkers, alteration-hands, etc.

    (*c*) Time- or piece-rates to cutters, pressers, underpressers.

B. Dressmaking.

(1) *Retail :*

    (*a*) Weekly time-rates.

    (*b*) Hourly time-rates.

    (*c*) Piece-rates. Not very common, owing to the greater importance attached to quality of workmanship than to quantity of output.

(2) *Wholesale.*

    Mostly piece-rates, but less elaborate than in wholesale tailoring.

C. Other Wholesale Sections.
As for wholesale dressmaking.

APPENDIX IIIA

Example of " Log "-rates

There are said to be about 300 " logs " in operation in the tailoring trade in Great Britain, but the great majority are purely local and merely embody slight modifications of the

O

well-known " logs," such as the London " log," the Lancashire " log " and the Scottish " log."

One of the great difficulties associated with payment by " log " lies in the problem of equating the " log " allowance with clock-times.

In the following Table will be found—

(1) A typical set of " log "-times, namely those fixed by the Scottish " log " as it stood in 1924, for the processes in making up a lounge jacket, firstly where the garment is made by hand throughout, and secondly where certain processes are made by machine. The item " deduct for third class " refers to the fact that the jacket in question is supposed to be made of " third-class " material.

(2) The payment that would be received for the jacket by a man working to the " log " at the rate of 9d. per log-hour, which was the rate current in 1924 in certain towns in Scotland.

(3) The *actual clock-times* for the same processes as fixed by a Joint Negotiating Committee of the Scottish Federation of Merchant Tailors and the Tailors' and Garment Workers' Trade Union.

(4) The payment that would be received for the jacket by a man working at a piece-work basis-time rate of 1s. 4½d. per hour, which was the Trade Board minimum rate in 1924 in the same towns.

It will be noted—

(a) That the relation between corresponding figures in columns (1) and (3) (and therefore, of course, in columns (2) and (4) also) is by no means a constant one. For instance, the clock-time for the item " Two holes and buttons on each cuff " is as much as eight-ninths of the log-time, whereas for the item " cutting, stitching and passing collar " it is only one-third of the clock-time. This feature of the log is particularly undesirable where the log-rates in operation are so low as only to yield about the same rates as the Trade Board minima and makes the proper enforcement of these minima impossible.

(b) That in actual fact, in the case in question, the total payment under the " log " falls short of the Trade Board minimum rates on the basis of the Joint Committee's clock-times by some 12 per cent.

It is to amend such anomalies as the foregoing that it has been repeatedly proposed to substitute ordinary piece-rates for the various systems of log-payment.

LOUNGE JACKET (3RD CLASS)
HANDWORK (THROUGHOUT)

	1 Log-hours as per Time Statement		2 Price at 9d. per Log-hour		3 Log Equation (*i.e.* Clock-time)		4 Piece-rates at 1/4½ per hour	
ITEMS	Hrs.	Min.	s.	d.	Hrs.	Min.	s.	d.
Planning and Marking-in	...	30	0	4½	...	20	0	5½
Two outside pockets	3	...	2	3				
Flaps out and in, bottoms jetted	...	45	0	6¾	1	45	2	4¾
Canvas	...	30	0	4½	...	15	0	4¼
Side seams	...	45	0	6¾	...	25	0	6¾
Padding lapels, staying edges	...	45	0	6¾				
and bridles	...	15	0	2¼	...	30	0	8¼
Pressing canvas pockets and seams	...	30	0	4½	...	20	0	5½
Making facings	...	30	0	4½	...	15	0	4¼
Basting over, including back lining	1	...	0	9	...	38	0	10¼
Felling in all linings	1	15	0	11¼	...	45	1	0¼
Shoulder seams	...	30	0	4½	...	15	0	4¼
Making-up front edges (raw or bluff	1	30	1	1½	...	40	0	11
Five holes in forepart	1	15	0	11¼	1	...	1	4½
Three buttons in forepart	...	15	0	2¼	...	9	0	2¼
Making plain sleeves	2	30	1	10½	1	15	1	8¾
Putting in sleeves	2	...	1	6	1	20	1	10
Joining coat	...	30	0	4½	...	15	0	4¼
Cutting, stitching and padding collar	1	30	1	1½	...	30	0	8¼
Pressing and covering collar	1	15	0	11¼				
Putting on collar	1	15	0	11¼	1	15	1	8¾
Pressing-off breasts	1	...	0	9				
Pressing-off coat	...	45	0	6¾	1	...	1	4½
	24	...	18	0	12	52	17	8¼
Deduct for third class	5	...	3	9	...	...	...	...
START	19	...	14	3	12	52	17	8¼
EXTRAS								
Out-breast pocket	1	30	1	1½	...	45	1	0¼
In-breast pocket	1	...	0	9	...	30	0	8¼
Ticket pocket	...	45	0	6¾	...	22	0	6
Edges stitched	2	30	1	10½	1	15	1	8¾
Long roll	...	30	0	4½	...	15	0	4¼
Vent in back (not exceeding 12 ins.)	...	45	0	6¾	...	20	0	5½
Vent in cuffs (4 ins.)	...	30	0	4½	...	20	0	5½
Two holes and buttons on each cuff	...	45	0	6¾	...	40	0	11
Canvas in cuffs	...	15	0	2¼	...	10	0	2¾
Cuts in side, including lining	1	...	0	9	...	25	0	6¾
Haircloth through shoulder	1	...	0	9	...	30	0	8¼
Wadding in back scye, not exceeding 3 plies	...	30	0	4½	...	15	0	4¼
TOTAL	30	...	22	6	18	39	25	7¾

APPENDIX IV.—METHODS OF WORK IN THE RETAIL BESPOKE TAILORING TRADES

A. One man, one job (*i.e.* coat, vest and trousers made throughout by coat-hand, vest-hand and trouser-hand respectively). *This method is now very rare.*

B. One man, with a girl for the less skilled parts of the job.

C. One man, with two girls, working as a team. (Possibly one machinist to every three teams.)

B and *C* are known as " Dual systems," and are still common in the West End.

D. Team on subdivisional lines, comprising—

(*a*) Workroom foreman or manager.
(*b*) Section foreman (if shop large enough).
(*c*) Fitter-up.
(*d*) Basters.
(*e*) Machinists.
(*f*) Sewers (various grades).
(*g*) Button-holers.
(*h*) Pressers.
(*i*) Learners.

In cases *A* and *B* payment is usually made at log-rates. The London " log " allows 30 log-hours for a lounge-coat, or 24 if all the deductions for work done by machine are made.

In case *C* payment may be by time-rates or piece-rates, usually the latter.

In case *D* payment is usually by time. This is the method used by Jewish subcontractors.

[Definition by Ministry of Labour of the terms " worker " and " subcontractor " in the Tailoring trade :

In order to make it clear which persons engaged in the tailoring trade are subject to the jurisdiction of the Retail Bespoke Trade Board and which to that of the Ready-made and Wholesale Bespoke Trade Board, the Ministry of Labour has issued the following memorandum :

(1) When a merchant tailor supplies a garment direct to an individual wearer, and employs workers *either upon his*

own premises or the premises of the worker, the worker must be paid at Retail Bespoke Trade Board rates.

(2) When the tailor engages a person to make garments on his own premises, and that person employs others to assist him, the others are under the Retail Bespoke section. Whether the person so engaged is himself under the Board depends on whether he is a *worker or subcontractor*. (See Para. 5.)

(3) When the tailor owns three or more retail establishments and employs workers at a central depot, if this depot is a factory under the Factory Acts, the workers are under the Ready-made and Wholesale Bespoke Trade Board ; if it is not a factory they are under the Retail Bespoke Trade Board.

(4) A person engaged by a master tailor to make up a garment *on his own premises, who performs no work himself*, is a subcontractor to whom no Trade Board rates apply ; his employees are under the Wholesale Board.

(5) Where the person mentioned in (4) also works himself, the case is doubtful. If he is a *worker* he and his men are under the Retail Board ; if he is a subcontractor, his men are under the Wholesale Board and he himself under no board].

INDEX

ABERDEEN, 80
Africa, South, 2, 29, 49, 50
Ahrons, Miss, 198
Aliens Immigration Act, 169, 199
America, 20, 38, 49
Ancoats, 49
Anderson, Miss, 189, 196
Apprentices and Learners, 94 ff.,
  161 ff., 212
Artificial Silk, 29, 33, 66
Australia, 2, 39, 50

BABY-LINEN, 27, 30, 57, 81
Barker & Co., John, 18, 74
Barran & Co., John, 38 ff.
Basingstoke, 19, 36
Bath, 25, 60
Bedford, 161
Bethnal Green, 113
Birmingham, 25, 27, 33, 35 ff.
Blackburn, 53
Blouses, 38, 43, 47, 63, 78
Booth, Charles, 79, 172
Boots and shoes, 10, 65, 208
Bourne & Hollinsworth, 76
Boys' clothing, 24, 47
Bradford, 27, 46
Brislington, 6
Bristol, 6, 18, 25, 27, 34, 35, 44,
  59 ff., 174
Bromsgrove, 59
Brown & Haig, 54

CADBURY, MATHESON and SHANN,
  59, 176
Cambridge, 11
Caps, 35, 48, 52, 81, 88
Cardiff, 6, 27, 40, 62-3
Carlisle, 30
Cave Committee, 85 ff., 97 ff.
" Checking-out," 58, 123
Clerkenwell, 78
Coats, 12, 20-2, 199
Colchester, 19, 36, 67-8, 174
Collars, 12, 21, 30-32, 36, 51
Collett, Miss, 173
Compton, 78
Conditions of work, 16, 39, 43,
  46, 73, 78 ff., 172 ff., 195 ff.
Conley, 198

Contract Houses, 19
Cook, Son & Co., 18
Co-operative Wholesale Society,
  6, 18, 37, 48, 49, 59, 60, 62
Corduroys, 3, 19, 47
Cornwall, 7
Corsets, 6, 10, 52, 88, 174
Cotterell, A. S., 102
Cotton, 33, 35, 47
Craig, 128
Crewe, 6, 19, 55 ff.
Curzons Ltd., 16
" Cut, Make and Trim," 6, 16
Cutters, 12, 23
Cutters Union, 142
Cutting, 12, 20, 32

Daily Herald, 186
Daily News Exhibition, 31, 172,
  182
Daly, 178
" Dead-horse," 23, 122, 124
Denton, 53
Department Stores, 76
Derry, 30, 31, 52, 140
Desborough, 6
Dingle, Miss, 190
Donegal Tweed Co., 54
Drake, Barbara, 72 n., 172 n.
Dual system, 212
Dudley, 56
Duffield, Mr, 197
Dundee, 35, 80
Dungarees, 32, 37

EARNINGS, 207-8
  (See also Wages)
East Anglia, 19, 36, 67-9
East London, 8, 34, 77 ff.
East Midlands, 35, 63 ff.
Edinburgh, 11, 36, 40, 80
Employers' Associations, 45,
  87 ff., 146 ff.
Employers, Ignorant, 43
Evans, 197

FACTORIES, 3, 4, 18, 20 ff., 28,
  30, 32, 38 ff., 53, 74 ff., 151,
  173 ff.
Fashions, 24, 26, 29

Federation, General Workshops, 154-6, 168
Finchley, 71
Flannel, 31
Foreign competition, 157
Forewomen, 21
Forfar, 8
Fur and Fancy Feather Trade, 10, 89

GERRISH, AMES & SIMPKINS, 81
Glasgow, 11, 18, 25, 27, 30, 36, 46, 47, 52, 81 ff., 174
Gloucester, 35
Gym-slips, 25

HALIFAX, 27, 29, 35, 46-8
Hammond, J. L. & B., 122
Handicraft tailoring, 3, 4, 11, 12, 15, 36, 50, 70 ff., 200
Handkerchiefs, 27
Hanover Square, 42, 73
Harrods, 18, 74
Hart & Levy, 65
Hebden Bridge, 7, 18, 35, 46-8
Heron, T. M., 160
Hoffman Press, 20
Homework Committee, 85
Homeworkers, 32, 51, 59, 61, 82, 172 ff.
Hosiery, 10, 35
Housing conditions, 46, 57, 71, 81, 173, 195
Huddersfield, 35, 46-8, 64
Hull, 37
Hutchins, B. L., 180 n.
Hyams, 68

IPSWICH, 67-9
Ireland, 30, 36, 140
Irwin, Miss, 174, 176

JACKETS, Lounge, 211
Jays, 76
Jews, passim
Joint Stock, 38
Jumpers, 6, 26, 47

KAFIR trade, 18, 31, 38, 47
Kellaway, 161
Kelly, 195
Kettering, 18, 35, 63 ff.
Kingsley, Charles, 165

LABOUR market, 19, 45, 64
Lace, 10, 28, 35 n., 65-6
Ladies' tailoring, 12

Leicester, 18, 25, 35, 63 ff.
Lewis Ltd., 63
Limehouse, 77
Linen, 31
Little & Co., David, 40
Liverpool, 11, 27, 35, 40
" Living-in," 76
" Logs," 2, 90 ff., 116 ff., 209-11
London, passim
Londonderry, see Derry
Luton, 65

MACARTHUR, Miss, 175, 176
Mallon, J. J., 144
Manchester, passim
Mann, Tom, 138
Mantles, 21 n., 24-7, 36, 42, 49, 76, 81, 88 ff.
Marks, Mr, 200
Markets, 33, 38
Meiklejohn, Miss, 193
Millinery, 10, 27, 36, 88 ff.
Multiple Shops, 37, 40-2
Mytholmroyd, 47

NANTWICH, 55 ff.
Newcastle-under-Lyme, 35, 55 ff.
Newcastle-on-Tyne, 6, 11, 36 n., 40
New Cross, 78
Newport (Mon.), 62
Northampton, 27, 63 ff.
Norwich, 19, 36
Nottingham, 11, 25, 27, 28, 35, 40, 52, 63 ff.
Numbers in clothing trades, 205-7
Nuneaton, 56

OILSKINS, 68
Old Ford, 78
Outwork, 61, 81, 176, 179, 191 ff.
Overalls, 32, 47
Overlocking machines, 29
Overtime, 98, 115
Oxford, 11
Oxford Circus, 77
Oxford Street, 7

PAISLEY, 30
Paris, 24
Peck & Co., John, 54
Piece-rates, see Wages
Plymouth, 18, 35, 60, 62, 64, 86
Poole, B. W., 1 n.
Pooles, 71
Portsmouth, 11, 36, 86

RAILWAY factories, 6, 19, 55
Raincoats, 17, 35, 38, 44, 49, 78
Raw materials, 33
Reading, 30, 36
Royal Army Clothing Factory, 19
Rylands Ltd., 52

SADLER, Miss, 193
Salford, 48
Sanitary conditions, 199, 200
Sartorial Gazette, 1 *n.*
Scotland, 36, 80, 82, 90 ff.
Seasonal fluctuations, 4, 42
Selfridges, 18, 74
Sells, Dorothy, 97
Sewing-machines, 120
Sewings, 123
Sheffield, 6, 11, 36, 37
Shepherd's Bush, 71, 78
Shirts, 6, 30, 32, 35-8, 51, 55 ff.,
    62, 178 ff.
Sittings, 70, 200
Skirts, 12, 26, 43, 81
Sleeving machine, 22
Smith, Councillor, 54
Soho, 7, 36, 71, 72, 86, 179
South Wales, 33, 35, 62, 63
Southern Counties, 34, 36
Southwark, 30
Sowerby Bridge, 47
Squire, Miss, 173, 174
Stockport, 30, 148, 152
Strikes and lockouts, 129, 130 *n.*,
    136, 138 ff., 144
Stroud, 25, 35, 61
Subcontractors, 7, 15, 16, 37, 44,
    53, 74, 209, 212
Subdivisional system, 13, 14, 19,
    155
Sullivan, Mr, 186
Sweating, 3, 16, 25, 31, 32, 55,
    67, 81, 85, 172 ff.
Swedes, 15
Swindon, 60

TAILORING, Retail Bespoke, 11-
    17, 69 ff., 80, 87, 100 ff., 209 ff.
Tailoring, Wholesale, 17-24, 35,
    36

Tailoring, Wholesale Bespoke,
    17-24, 40, 41
Taunton, 30, 35, 60
Tawney, R. H., 48
Taylor, Miss, 124, 194, 196
Teamwork, 13, 14, 122
Time rates, *see* Wages
Tootal, Broadhurst, Lee & Co.,
    52
Trade Board Acts, 4, 83 ff.
Trade Boards rates, 83 *et passim*
Trade Boards, Appointed mem-
    bers, 91, 94, 95
Trade unions, 195 *et passim*
Tropical clothing, 6, 36, 67
Trousers, 12, 22, 42, 119

UNDERCLOTHING, 6, 27-30, 35,
    50 ff., 78 ff.
Unemployment and short-time,
    65-69, 114
Uniform clothing, 17
Uniforms, Court, 12

VINES, Miss, 173

WAGES, 83 ff., 209 ff., *et passim*
Wages, arrears of, 103
Wages, deductions from, 122 ff.
Waistcoats, 12, 22
Waiting-time, 23, 99, 122-3
Walsall, 35, 56
War Office, 6, 19
War, Great, 31, 32, 39, 40, 49,
    86 ff., 108 ff., 132 ff.
Webb, Sidney, 72
Webb, Mrs Sidney, 75
Wellingborough, 34, 63 ff.
West Ham, 113
West Midlands, 35, 55-9
West Riding, 34, 35, 46
" Whipping the cat," 2
Whitechapel, 74, 77 ff.
White goods, 30
Wool and Woollens, 33, 35
Woolwich, 78

YARMOUTH, 68

For Product Safety Concerns and Information please contact our EU
representative GPSR@taylorandfrancis.com Taylor & Francis Verlag GmbH,
Kaufingerstraße 24, 80331 München, Germany

Printed and bound by CPI Group (UK) Ltd, Croydon, CR0 4YY
08/05/2025
01864469-0001